LEAN MACHINES

LEARNING FROM THE LEADERS OF THE NEXT INDUSTRIAL REVOLUTION

By Richard A. McCormack

Editor & Publisher
Manufacturing News

A Lean Strategy Is The Only One That Has An Across-The-Board Impact

	Cost	Asset Efficiency		Growth			Valuation Premium	Est. of Penetration
		Plant & Equipmt.	Inventory	Quality	Speed	Delivery		
Lean Strategies	●	●	●	●	●	●	●	<5%
Restructuring	◖	◖						75%
Cost Reduction Programs	◖							100%
Traditional TQM	◖			◖				50%
Six Sigma	◖	◖		●	◖	◖	◖	10%
Other Operational Improvement Methodologies (Big 5; Costanza; McKinsey)	◖	◖	◖		◖	◖		15%

● full impact

◖ partial impact

(Source: Cliff Ransom, Director of Research, Janney Montgomery Scott LLC)

PUBLISHERS & PRODUCERS

Copyright 2002, Richard A. McCormack
Publishers & Producers
P.O. Box 36
Annandale, VA 22003
703-750-2664
On the Web at: http://www.manufacturingnews.com
ISBN 0-9722407-0-5

For information on corporate and academic discounted bulk purchases, call
703-750-2664.

Library of Congress Cataloging-in-Publication Data

McCormack, Richard A.
  Lean Machines, learning from the leaders of the next industrial revolution /
  Interviews with Alcoa, Delphi, Toyota, Boeing, Wiremold, Barry Controls,
  Lockheed Martin, Freudenberg-NOK, Exide Technologies, BMA, Lean
  Enterprise Institute, Danaher/Lean Horizons, Warner Robins AFB, Janney
  Montgomery Scott LLC, HON Industries/Simpler Consulting
  1. Lean manufacturing; new management and production system.

Cover art is from Danaher Corp.'s 2001 Annual Report.

PUBLISHERS & PRODUCERS

CONTENTS

INTRODUCTION

Having covered industry, science and technology as a journalist for the past 20 years, I have been a recipient of marketing and PR hype from those promoting the latest technical "breakthroughs" and business fads. Superconductivity, cold fusion, massively parallel processing supercomputers, video on demand, business process reengineering, B2B trading exchanges and e-commerce were all going to "revolutionize" the world. Perhaps.

Now when I hear the word revolutionary (or "breakthrough") to describe the latest technology, software or business system, I cower.

Yet the "revolutionary" moniker can be applied to one Japanese business system that has proven itself in practice: Lean. The companies that have embraced the concept have undergone a profound transformation and in many cases are defeating competitors that have not yet taken the plunge.

Companies deploying the lean concepts of building-to-order (pull) and continuous improvement (kaizen) are reducing waste, improving quality, introducing more products, creating a positive working environment, winning orders and riding out lulls in the economy. These companies — like Dell, Toyota, Alcoa and Wiremold — are outperforming their competitors in most every measure.

In a sense, lean is misnamed. To the uninitiated, it sounds like another cost-cutting program. When the professional people I know who are not involved in the industrial community ask me about it, I tell them that lean manufacturing is a system based on producing a product only after an order is received. Instead of building to inventory or building to a sales forecast, lean is a system of building to a customer's specific order. The idea makes their brain spin a bit because they realize intuitively that such a system requires a reorientation of all aspects of a company's operations.

Making the leap from understanding the concept to implementing it is not easy. Ask the practitioners at the best lean companies — including Toyota, which invented the concept and has been at it for 50 years — if they have been successful and they humbly admit that they are only scratching the surface of a system that is vastly superior to mass production or any other method of running a business enterprise.

A few U.S. companies are now almost a decade into applying the lean principles that were first articulated to a worldwide audience in the 1991 best-selling book *The Machine That Changed The World*. Their success can be emulated by tens of thousands of companies that don't yet understand the concept, but must learn soon or risk not surviving the next economic downturn.

A journalist's job is to take the spoken word and write it down. This is a unique task, and not an altogether easy one, as I have learned over the past 20 years.

I like question-and-answer articles with people who are as passionate about a subject as I am. Experts who have spent their lives ingrained within a discipline are typically unique characters and when they speak freely they do not have to worry about grammar, punctuation, style, composition and all the other headaches of writing. Q&As often provide the most enlightening and fruitful of reading.

Over the past 18 months, I have interviewed individuals who were recommended to me by the most knowledgeable lean experts. These same people have also helped by providing me with questions that could shed light on the perplexing and largely unexplored aspects of a lean implementation.

A number of themes run throughout the interviews in this book. In many cases, we have edited out repetitive concepts, leaving them to be described by the person who is the most articulate on the subject.

We are at the beginning of a new era in production. It is exciting and the people interviewed in *Lean Machines* share a deep and infectious enthusiasm for the topic. They are the first generation of Americans taking the intellectual plunge to understand and apply a fundamentally simple yet difficult concept that truly — and without hyperbole — holds the promise of achieving the next industrial revolution.

— *Richard McCormack*

About The Author:

Richard McCormack is editor and publisher of *Manufacturing News*, a publication created in 1994 that is read by executives in industry, government and academia on five continents. Prior to creating *Manufacturing News*, he was founding editor of *New Technology Week* and *High Performance Computing and Communications Week*. Prior to that, he was editor of *The Energy Daily*.

McCormack has won awards for investigative, analytical and interpretive reporting. Over the course of his career, he has interviewed thousands of business executives, politicians, workers and scientists including Seymour Cray, inventor of the supercomputer; Robert Noyce, inventor of the integrated circuit; Edward Teller, inventor of the thermonuclear bomb; and Douglas Engelbart, inventor of the computer mouse.

TOYOTA MOTOR CORP.

Best-selling business books have been written about the Toyota Production System (TPS) developed by Eiji Toyoda and Taiichi Ohno shortly after WW II. The Harvard Business School has studied it in depth. Companies from across the entire spectrum of the industrial world have emulated the system, which is based upon just-in-time production, the elimination of waste and continuous improvement, with striking results.

Toyota's point man on TPS in America is Ken Kreafle, vice president of quality at Toyota's Georgetown, Kentucky, production facility.

Many companies think they can purchase their success like a piece of equipment.

Toyota did not start with the lean tools.

What makes it so hard for a company that is not deploying these techniques to come up to full speed on a Toyota Production System or a lean production system?

KREAFLE: [*Lean Thinking* author] Jim Womack says Toyota people are marinated in this TPS thing, but for other companies, it's a cultural change, which means you have to look right at the top of the company.

Many companies think they can hire consultants and purchase their success like a piece of equipment. They spend a lot of money and try to activate a lot of things in their company, but the people at the top are not really supporting the cultural changes. You can tell this by what they approve and what they don't approve. They remove themselves from it and are maintaining their old way of doing business and expecting a change to happen. It doesn't work.

The coaching I give companies that are trying to change is there is a big distinction between the principles of the Toyota Production System and the tools of the Toyota Production System. Most people can spout kanban and andon systems, but those are the tools — that is the end point of a string of thinking.

Most people go to the hardware side of issues and they install an andon system or a kanban system and they hear about the mechanics of a kaizen system and put it into their plant. But the softer side of management — the thinking side — hasn't changed to support and nurture those activities.

I try to explain to them that Toyota did not start with an andon system. It didn't start with any of those things. The andon system is very basic — it relentlessly continues to say, do not pass a defect onto the next person.

How do we do that? Eventually we had to give the workers some way of highlighting a problem and that became the andon tool. The tools are visible; it's what people see and it's what people read about. But without installing the thinking — the principles of it — they cannot be developed or maintained in a normal plant.

How much of the success of the TPS is focused on management?

KREAFLE: NUMMI, one of our sister plants, was a GM plant. It was shut down and they basically rehired under the new Toyota Production System from the same pool of people who were there under the old GM system. Today, NUMMI is a very formidable company. That is an example of where you take the same workforce that was managed one way and basically change the management system and, boom, right out of the shoot, they were a TPS-functioning company.

How hard is it to change an old-line management mentality?
KREAFLE: The best successes I've seen myself are in small companies where the very top people themselves study it and introduce it. When Dennis Pawley started the Chrysler Operating System, he himself eventually taught the Chrysler Operating System. That is so powerful because when he teaches it he not only says something to the people, but it affects the decisions he makes in the daily business policies and procedural approval and behaviors, the tolerances and temperances that are necessary to balance the system. He then makes his own adjustments and teaches it to his upper management. I don't know what's happened since he left the Chrysler organization, but I would imagine that could have taken a step backwards. I'm not sure.

What are the differences between TPS and the production systems run by your competitors?
KREAFLE: The characteristics of one system model to another are so subtle that it's sometimes hard to see. The main difference in non-TPS companies is there is a tendency for management not only to do problem solving but also do method selection — the how are we going to do it. In a TPS company, we're trying to involve the strengths of our workforce in method development.

Basically, Toyota dispersed all of the elements of industrial engineering, which used to be the private domain of upper management, down to the worker. We taught it to them and tried to get all of them working on efficiency improvements.

The Toyota Production System is not something that is in the boss's head for the employees to extract, but it is on paper. It is approved and taught to employees by management. TPS is not the "five who" analysis to root blame, but the "five why" analysis to root cause.

People have a deep inner sense of what is correct. The true leader brings it out. Does anyone not see more capabilities and capacity in their company's people than is actually being used?

It takes trust for management to give up control.
KREAFLE: It switches management from being a problem-solving, method-generator to target generating, coaching and mentoring. That's where quite often there is failure. It is difficult for a company that has traditionally been run by management that is more decision-method driven to change their habits and release those activities to their people.

That's why the successes I've seen have been in smaller supplier companies where this transformation occurs in management and then takes root in the worker side.

The very top people themselves study it.

TPS is not something that is in the boss's head for the employees to extract.

Is it inevitable that lean will become the dominant form of operation for companies in order for them to compete?

KREAFLE: No, I don't think so. Ford is successful and it has a different model they have followed for quite a while. But Ford, GM and Chrysler are looking at a very large turnover in their workforce and management in the very near future. Many, many people are going to retire. Coming in behind them is going to be the X-Generation and the X-Generation wants this degree of involvement.

For us, it's the Toyota Production System, but some concept that blends this involvement of the workers into the daily business is going to be essential for survival with the next generation.

Involvement of the workers in the daily business is going to be essential.

How will the Toyota Production System evolve over the next decade?

KREAFLE: The basic elements of the system are somewhat timeless. That's dangerous to say because nothing is timeless. The system evolves. But the thing that is really going to be a big change for us is to learn how to use the power of computers, the Internet and Intranets in our business.

Can the Toyota Production System adapt to a make-to-order manufacturing system that might soon come about thanks to the Internet?

KREAFLE: We're looking at that. How fast we're going to get there and who's going to get there first, we're all chancing it. We have to look at how people still buy cars, because some of my study of the Internet is that some things that seemed to show real promise like food shopping don't seem to be working on the Internet. People still like to feel and touch their vegetables.

One of the reasons why inventory exists with cars is for people to look at and test and sample and fall into the one they want. At the very instant they fall into the one they want, the current market is they drive away. The concept of the three-day car is good, but I'm not sure if our customers want to wait three days.

Is TPS capable of handling potentially radical change?

KREAFLE: The basic core elements, yes, because the Toyota Production System is basic. What I question is whether the company has enough futuristic thinking to be preparing the technologies that are necessary for the future. That's a real point of concern with any company because you don't know where it's going.

A larger number of people can tackle problems.

One of the elements of TPS is that more and more people are engaged in running the business day to day. Whenever a problem occurs, we have the ability to download these problems to a larger number of people rather than trying to cluster with a smaller group of people trying to make a decision.

New model changes and expansions weaken the implementation of the Toyota Production System.

Every company that is successful gives their people something rock solid to believe in.

How hard is it for a company to come up to speed on a lean production system? Is there a lot to learn?

KREAFLE: The more significant time is spent not in learning but in the maintenance of the system. After they get into it many people refer to it as being just common sense and logic because one of the main characteristics of TPS is getting your workforce more involved. Getting people involved means you generate a system that requires a lot of maintenance. For Toyota, new model changes and expansions weaken the implementation of the Toyota Production System because we're bringing in new people or moving people. So rebuilding those habits is a high-maintenance system.

Does a lean production system naturally atrophy over time?

KREAFLE: What I'm talking about is rebalancing. You're always trying to balance on an orientation toward safety, quality, and the elements of efficiency with cost being one of them. During the course of a major model change, more of the attention is on maintaining quality. During that time, you might not exercise as much of the cost and productivity improvements and kaizen activities and they become a little weaker and less ingrained. You have to hold the quality and then go back and re-ignite the activities for improvements in cost, productivity, direct run and other activities.

Does TPS have more of a focus on productivity or quality?

KREAFLE: Every company that I've seen and studied that is successful gives their people something rock solid to believe in and our company believes in the product quality of our vehicle. Quality takes a tremendous focus and a lot of energy and effort. No one can do everything all the time. At periods of change, our balance of human effort and activity will focus toward quality. Once we get that phase stable, we rekindle and reactivate the activities toward making it more efficient.

Have you learned some things that you can apply to the next model introductions so that you keep the lean focus throughout the process of introducing a new vehicle?

KREAFLE: Absolutely. We talk about standard work, which is like scientific experimentation. As you do an experiment you keep records of what worked and what didn't work. Toyota emphasizes reflection-types of activities after projects. Every company reflects on past projects, but how much energy do you really put into it? How many true activities are utilized? And does it cascade into the next project? Our system doctrines say you not only reflect but learn and cascade those activities into your next project.

Every single phase is analyzed and each is adjusted a little bit. Basically we're doing what the whole industry is doing in that we're getting more and more of our manufacturing people involved in the early stages of model development. We are constantly reflecting on how to get earlier involvement to find problems not only with design but also with manufacturing.

How important now is it for your suppliers to get on board and become a similar type of organization? Is the supply chain's adoption of TPS where the savings are going to come for Toyota?

KREAFLE: We're asking them to engage in TPS. One of my feelings about industry right now is Americans have a tendency to repackage the same thing under different names and different acronyms such as QS 9000 or ISO 14001. As rudimentary as you can get, you have to say what you're going to do, and do what you're going to say. TPS says analyze what you did and make it better with enough managerial discipline to bar your ego a little bit [by saying] "Let's not have it my way."

I refer to it as management by evolution rather than management by revolution. Constant small improvement is one of our doctrines. A lot of the words that guide the behavior is an evolutionary step by step rather than let's jump in and make a monumental revolutionary change. TPS is very methodical and progressive.

Japan has been criticized for this evolutionary approach to change which has hurt its economy while U.S. technology companies took the revolutionary approach with great success. Can the evolutionary approach backfire on Toyota?

KREAFLE: When I say evolutionary, I'm referring to a sense of feeling of what it's like to be in the Toyota organization. We're trying to make the system stronger and stronger. When people are talking about revolutions they are not TPS system revolutions, but they are major shifts in the industry or they are tremendously large steps in indicators such as hours per vehicle. Some of those metrics indicate very large changes.

TPS is not quick fixes by decree of management. Instead, no quick fixes exist to the real root cause and temporary controls are okay.

But what I'm talking about is like the game book for a football team. We continue to try to improve the game book. Even though you try to improve the game book, you still have to keep exercising the execution of that. So with that as our game strategy, we're in the industrial automotive arena that is going to experience big changes. I can almost be ridiculous when I talk about how big a change that is going to happen in this industry. You can consider everything from global positioning systems to wireless cars to cars being plastic and no one doubts that any more.

There is a metamorphosis that is going to happen in the automobile industry in five to 10 years. Who would have ever thought the Post Office would be threatened for business. But e-mail is doing that. The digital camera is replacing Kodak film. Those are revolutions. There is no reason to believe the auto industry is going to escape that.

For Toyota, we're trying to evolve and generate the strength in our

Constant small improvement is one of our doctrines.

TPS is not quick fixes by decree of management.

system so that when we have the monumental target to go after, we have the strength and implementation of our system strong enough to react to it faster than our competition.

Toyota is well ahead of other auto companies — evidence the early introduction of the hybrid Prius.

KREAFLE: That only scratches the surface of the changes in vehicles that are going to come about. By 2003, zero-emission cars are required in California. Cradle-to-grave responsibility is certainly going to come here.

Why hasn't any other automobile company yet caught Toyota?

KREAFLE: Because of our long-term adherence to the system. Toyota has generated a very high degree of cross-company adherence to it and that generates managerial strength and a tremendous amount of consistency. The real benchmark for Toyota quality is vehicle-to-vehicle-to-vehicle consistency. If you took any one of our vehicles and any one of our competitors', you could probably find any one that out-performs ours, but if you look at the variation between our vehicles and the variation of our competition, then it's a different story.

Does Toyota achieve Six-Sigma quality?

KREAFLE: Basically, I would say that because of our evolutionary concept, whatever we were doing becomes the benchmark for what we do next. We try to hold onto whatever we were doing so that it becomes maintainable and it is the new steady state. We're not moving from one chance occurrence to another. We're moving from one steady state to the next steady state.

Can you define the Toyota Production System?

KREAFLE: It is a way of thinking. It is a way of thinking about waste elimination that improves operating efficiency. It is divided into principles and tools like andon and kanban systems. Some of the principles include highlighting problems when and where they happen and the conditions in which they occurred. They include constant small improvements by focusing on the work that each individual does and the idea that management must change first. When management buys into the process then and only then should it take it to the people with a plan on how and when to introduce new things. The follow up will determine success.

Are there other basic principles that are not well understood by most companies?

KREAFLE: One is that only the teacher can fail. Another is that there are no job descriptions in the Toyota Production System. The delineation of what people do is determined by their training. And finally, communications are the responsibility of the sender not the receiver, which is similar to the principle of only the teacher can fail.

We're moving from one steady state to the next steady state.

Only the teacher can fail.

TPS tools show either normal or abnormal operating conditions.

What are the specific tools of the Toyota Production System?

KREAFLE: Just-in-time, jidoka, kanban, heijunka, kaizen, standard work, takt time, work sequence and standard in-process stock are some of them. Jidoka and just-in-time are the two pillars in which the structure of the TPS system is supported.

TPS tools are developed to show either normal or abnormal operating conditions. A normal operating condition meets a standard or agreed procedure. Normal operating conditions still require kaizen activities involving problem solving that incorporate reference to standards, five why analysis, root-cause identification and countermeasure development. An abnormal operating condition does not meet a standard or agreed procedure and goes through the same problem solving activity. The goal is to reach standardization for the creation of normal operating conditions.

The Toyota Production System is focused on people. They know what is expected of them and they are able to influence and correct problems. They also help develop methods to keep problems from returning. We focus on procedures and not on results, as in traditional companies. The method used to obtain results is important and constantly under consideration for improvement. As a way of thinking, TPS points out what is a normal condition and what is an abnormal condition.

LOCKHEED MARTIN CORP.

One of the early adopters of lean in the United States was Pratt & Whitney, and a foot soldier in that company's quest to improve itself was a then young Michael Joyce, who is corporate vice president of operating excellence in charge of LM21, the lean transformation initiative taking place at Lockheed Martin. While at Pratt & Whitney, Joyce worked and studied with the masters of the Toyota Production System brought into the company by United Technologies chairman George David, who had long understood the workings of Japan's industrial behemoths.

Prior to joining Lockheed Martin, Joyce was vice president for manufacturing at AlliedSignal Aerospace. He has served on the board at the Massachusetts Institute of Technology's Lean Aerospace Initiative and is on the Board of Governors for the Shingo Prize for Excellence in Manufacturing.

Understand work from the bottom up.

I want you to write down what the operator is doing right now.

You studied lean manufacturing at Pratt & Whitney under some of the Japanese masters. What did you learn?

JOYCE: The best lesson I got out of the Japanese management philosophy — the hands-on, every-day philosophy — is they do a much better job of understanding work from the bottom up. The top down they do well, but they do the bottom up exceptionally well. We have core skills at the top — program management and defining work tasks — but we have blind spots in really understanding bottom-up thinking.

Japanese manufacturers use video cameras a great deal in analyzing the way people move in their work cells. They benchmark against the video and then go back and perfect their motions.

JOYCE: It feeds into their strategy and philosophy which is, "Go do and then let's talk about it."

When the Japanese guys first showed up [at Pratt & Whitney] we were thinking, "Oh God, here come these automotive guys to tell us how to build jet engines. What do they know about jet engines and the quality levels that are required?" We had all the excuses. You can't pull a jet engine off to the side of the road if something breaks at 40,000 feet.

The Japanese guys showed up and we told them we had some problems. Chihiro [Nakao of the Shingijutsu consulting group], who was great at this, would then say, "Here's your clip board. Here's your pen. Let's go down to the floor and take a look at what's really happening."

He'd drag you down and say, "Stand there and watch. Don't talk to anybody. Just stand there and watch. I want you to write down what the operator is doing right now."

It was very in-your-face, go look at what's happening right now and confront that ugly reality because the ugly reality is the guy is off looking for tools.

Then he said the method for capturing what is actually happening is a video camera. Here is your video camera. Capture all of it and now sit your butt in that chair and turn that camera on and to the second tell me if what's going on is what you think should be happening. That is the only thing that matters.

But Americans don't want to step on people's toes. They don't want to feel like they're hovering over workers with video cameras assessing their every move. We want to let people do their own jobs and defer to them even though what they are producing is not very good.

JOYCE: One of the things I instituted here is that when we do quarterly reviews I insisted that [former Lockheed Martin president and COO of Aeronautics Sector] Mickey [Blackwell] go down to the floor and take a look for himself. Most CEOs couldn't even tell you where the product gets made.

That kind of coaching you never have to give to a Japanese manager. When a Japanese CEO comes to a facility, the first place he goes is to the factory. He already knows where the inspection department is — you don't have to show it to him.

In many American companies, you have to go down pretty far into an organization before you can actually ask somebody where they inspect things and they know where it is. We started putting those kinds of cultural changes in place and it's paying off. That kind of attention travels fast.

The best companies have their own bumper stickers for excellence, whether it be Six Sigma quality, TQM or continuous improvement. Why did Lockheed Martin adopt lean?

JOYCE: When I interviewed for this job, Mickey was telling me about Andy Grove's book *Only the Paranoid Survive*, which is a great book. But I sent him back James Womack's book [*Lean Thinking*] and said if you're serious about this, this is the book that does the best.

Womack has done a great job of capturing Toyota's system. We made the book required reading for everybody. I bought thousands of copies and distributed it to everybody. I paid his mortgage for him.

One of the problems with lean or agile is that everyone tries to rationalize what they are already doing as being lean. They say we've been doing lean for 15 years. But when you look at it, they haven't done anything.

So rather than leave it random, we said you can pick 10 different ways to do this, but let's just pick one and let's start talking one language.

Did you have any desire to adopt Eli Goldratt's work?

JOYCE: I went through all of Goldratt's stuff and it's good but what I finally came to realize from the Toyota folks is that it's only a subset of the total. He got into the theory of constraints. GE went down that road for a while, but it is a subset of the total.

Here's what I learned from the Japanese lean guys. You run things to a concept called takt time and anything that can't make the takt time becomes a constraint and by definition needs to be fixed. However, if you can move one part of the process and save ten seconds of work, why don't you do it? Just do it.

Most CEOs couldn't even tell you where the product gets made.

We made "Lean Thinking" required reading for everybody.

Do you know how much 10 seconds costs in this factory?

We're different.

"Give me a crowbar. I want a crowbar right now."

If you're working with the constraint theory, if it's not a constraint and it's not on a critical path, who cares, even if you just saved 10 seconds. The Japanese guys would say, "Do you know how much 10 seconds costs in this factory?" They actually have you go out and calculate how much it costs to run the factory for every second. Do you know what 10 seconds is worth?

Goldratt added to the table, but I got completely more blown away when the Toyota guys came in and gave me the real nuts and bolts. For the most part, it's Toyota that is way ahead.

One of the things I've often heard about the defense industry is that it has to get away from the idea that it is different. What do you think?

JOYCE: I did that with our sensei Yoshio Oba [of Shingijutsu]. I'd say, "We're different, you don't understand what we're doing here at Pratt." He'd say, "Grab your notebook, let's go the floor and let's go talk about how different you are. Stand here and watch them and take notes. Now let's talk about what we can do. Now go do it. Now let's sit down and talk about how different you are."

What is the essence of lean manufacturing at Lockheed Martin?

JOYCE: What lean boils down to is the study of work. What are the wasted portions of any work that we do in the office or factory? The tough part is you have to have the courage to acknowledge that there is waste and then you have to have the tenacity to go do something about it.

The Toyota guys used the phrase "Just Do It" long before Nike. Oba used to have the best technique that I've ever come across. There are all kinds of reasons why you can't get something done. For instance, you may want to move a machine but you don't have an EPA permit to put a new stack through the ceiling and you have to get regulatory approval or other such excuses.

Oba used to say, "Go and write them all down on a piece of paper and let's have a meeting." So we'd write them down on a piece of paper and come to the meeting and he said, "Let me see the list." He'd take the list and he'd say, "I own the list now. Go do it."

The Toyota guys had a spirit that I really admire. We'd have machines the size of this room and we'd say this machine is in the wrong place. We decided after we studied it that the best place for it was over there. They say, "It's now Thursday, one o'clock. By Monday morning at seven o'clock, machine over there."

Everybody would be standing around looking at each other saying you've got to be nuts, and he'd say, "Give me a crowbar, I want a crowbar right now. I'll move it. Why aren't you moving the machine right now. Time is ticking." We'd be off doing planning and calling maintenance.

One of the best stories is about [Chihiro] Nakao [of the Shingijutsu consulting group] at an Otis facility in Brazil for UTC because [UTC chairman George] David had this going on throughout the corporation.

Nakao wanted a machine moved *now* and he's grabbing a crowbar on the floor saying, "I want this machine moved *now*." He's doing this with a lot of theatrics because they really try to engage you on an emotional level. One of the things I learned is that 20 percent of this is intellectual and 80 percent is emotional.

Nakao is making a huge fuss on the floor because people aren't moving. They summon the general manager of the plant down to the floor who asks what's going on and they explain to him that this guy wants to move this machine, but there is a wall in the way and he wants to move it now.

Nakao goes over and knocks on the wall and he jumps on a forklift truck in front of the GM and drives it through the wall and gets off the truck and he says, "Now no wall. Move the machine."

It's intense, but it is urgent.

Look, if this machine is better over here, then move it now while we are sitting here. Let's not debate it. Let's not talk about it because we can learn from that. Maybe it isn't better there and it's better someplace else, but we'll have it done four times before the day is over.

We had to move a machine that was honest-to-God as big as this room that did a thing called flame spray which had plasma sprayed on metal parts with gas lines and a controlled environment. And he says, "It's Friday, I want it over there by Monday."

And you stand there and scratch your head and say I don't know how we're going to do this. This is impossible. But they challenge you to get creative. So we got all of the people who had been working on that machine for 20 years and we said here is the challenge, we have to move it over there by Monday, what are we going to do?

People started volunteering information, saying, "One time we had to go in and repair the darn thing and at first we thought we were going to have to take it apart and then when the mechanic came in we decided we didn't have to take it apart because we could block it here, sling it and tie it off. Why don't we not take it apart, and just block it, sling it and tackle it like we did before?"

So we shut off all the power and cut all the lines that came to it, we put a big strap around it, took it off the floor and started moving it like you move a house. We slid it a foot, stopped, went in and took a look at everything. It was okay. Slid it another foot and by Monday we had the thing running. It felt like we had been there a month.

Q: What was the benefit of moving it?
JOYCE: We took the cycle time to make a product from five weeks to one day just by reconfiguring the work area around the idea of flow. We knew it was absolute waste to put parts in and out of boxes and transport them down the aisle.

We had to do something about it. The only way to get out of all this boxing and inventory was by moving the machine.

We had to move a machine that was honest-to-God as big as this room.

You can move anything in days. It's not that hard.

We had machinery that had been in place since 1952 when the building went up because it's so big. You get it into your mind that you can't move this stuff. But once you clear that obstacle and you have a couple of victories under your belt, you convince yourself that you can move anything in days. It's not that hard. But that is a mental block. People don't think that way with big equipment.

That's especially true when you're making big products.
JOYCE: We were producing at high volume with lots of spares and we couldn't be out of production. But we blew through all the bull: no engineering studies; no ROI calculations; nothing that was top down. We blow through all of that by saying, "Give me the crowbar, I'll do it myself."

If I had to bumper sticker this whole exercise, it's both bottom-up and top-down. When you step back and look at it, it is system engineering — how you do work in the totality of a system

Why is Womack's work so appealing to you?
JOYCE: The reason I like using Womack is that he has been able to describe what is behind the Toyota system and the idea of value and value stream. Do you know all the detailed steps required to deliver value to the customer?

Toyota settled the score on looking at complicated systems and determined that to optimize for efficiency, what takes precedent is flow. That is the real requirement. Can you optimize the flow?

That takes on a lot of manifestations; one is the flow of a bit of data that is trying to become a decision and an action. For making products, the work system has to be set up so that once you commit to creating a product the part doesn't stop moving until it's done. It takes months for us to build stuff because we have not latched on to optimizing the work system for flow.

Do you know all the detailed steps required to deliver value to the customer?

If you're going to optimize for flow, then tell me again why I'm taking the parts coming out of this machine the size of a room, putting them into a box, shipping them somewhere else, taking them out again, working on them and shipping them back? That doesn't sound like it is optimized for flow. You have to do better than that. If you say we can optimize for flow but it's going to force us to reconfigure the floor, what are you waiting for? You have until Monday, one o'clock. Go ahead, reconfigure the floor.

Now you have Dell and other companies building to order. They don't manufacture the product until they have the order in hand and they can deliver in four days.
JOYCE: That is the fourth principle Womack hits upon. He calls it pull because when you drop the cycle times down you get rid of all the guesswork about what is really needed.

There have been hundreds of scientific studies and books written on the art of forecasting. It's a black science. It's like trying to predict the stock market. If you can really get the thing optimized for flow and collapse the cycle down, you can go to a pull system.

You don't have to forecast. You just have to guarantee a delivery cycle that is X which is less than your cycle time. So the name of the game is crush your cycle time.

The name of the game is crush your cycle time.

How do you introduce lean manufacturing at Lockheed Martin?

JOYCE: I tell people that there are three levels of doing this. It's like a Nintendo game; as you go to the next level, it gets a little tougher.

The lean principles are the first. It's 20 percent intellectual. You can get this pretty quick. It makes sense. The next level is the tactical elements of how you do it. Here is what Toyota teaches: takt, flow, pull — over and over again. They drill that into you. It's very hands on, very step by step. You can't get lean without dragging yourself through learning what you have to do to make it happen.

The third level is the most challenging, it's the why you are doing it. It says you understand what it's all about and how to do it and you understand the unique thing that is your business. Now what are you going to do to create something nobody else has done? There is no book yet written on how you build a lean fighter weapons system.

The natural reaction of everybody when they go through it is this is not me. This is somebody else. This is an operations thing. This is not made for finance.

The challenge is not to take the off ramp.

The challenge is not to take the off ramp. The challenge is to stay on the path and say I'm going to force myself to figure out a way to apply this to what I do. And then you'll make some real breakthroughs.

The implementation plan has to stress the idea of top down, bottom up. You have to have leadership at the process-owner levels. But the reality is it happens from the bottom up. You have to critically evaluate how you do work, attack the system and get people excited about wanting to be part of it because it can be exciting. But it can also be perceived as being threatening, especially on a personal level.

How hard is it to tell operators that they're doing this for their own good? Don't they come back at you and say, "Oh, yeah, sure"?

JOYCE: It's hard to overcome if you do it wrong, and it's easy to do wrong. I just read recently about a plant manager going to the factory to an all-hands meeting and announcing that the company was undertaking a new productivity initiative. He said, "We have people working this and they'll be in your area helping you improve productivity."

It's hard to overcome if you do it wrong.

He went back to his office and about three hours later a bunch of hourly people showed up in his office. They walked right in and started rearranging his furniture and they said, "Don't you worry, this is going to make you more productive." Then they walked out. He got the point pretty quickly.

It doesn't really work in a command-and-control military system, which I'm sure is prevalent in a defense contractor simply because so many people working here come from a military background.

JOYCE: What I've learned in doing this is you have to work it from the bottom up. If you don't, it opens too many trap doors and it's going to kill you later. When you get people engaged and things happen, the excitement level is infectious.

We went down [to Georgia] and in three days we completely rebuilt an F-22 build area and took half of the labor out. The people who worked in the area were ecstatic.

It was a two-station platform in which the aircraft is in partial build and there were two stations — up and down. You had to go up and down the platform to get tools and materials. It worked, but they were going up and down the stairs hundreds of times per day and we captured it on the video. We asked, "Why don't we put all of your stuff up top?" They said the upper platform was too small and the drawings and specs were down below.

We said the platform has to get bigger and everything you need has to be up on the platform. If you need a computer up there, we'll put a computer up here. Anything you need let's put up there. We told everybody that if you need a platform built, grab a piece of sheet metal, here's the welding torch and go put it up. I don't need to see an ROI, just get out there and do it.

In three days they rebuilt the whole thing. This was a cramped workspace and the operators in the area hated it. They hated having to go chase everything. They love it now. The next time we suggested they do something, you couldn't hold them back with a stick. They would say, "I've been complaining about this for years and now in three days it happened. What are we going to do next? I want to do this again."

So it is infectious once you get people involved in doing it.

Productivity growth means you produce more products with less labor hours and you need fewer workers. Do workers see it as a threat to their jobs?

JOYCE: It's a real concern and you are going to freak people out if you tell them they have to do more work. They can buy into it if you put it in a global sense by asking them how to keep manufacturing jobs in the U.S. The only way to grow your business, add more jobs and get customers is with cost-effective prices. Most people can buy into that.

When you get down to the local level, the name of the game is how do you use labor productively? If you take the labor out, you have something else for them to do. Some of the things we're looking into is insourcing work that used to get outsourced.

So we tell people that we have to be the best aircraft company in the world so that we can win things like the Joint Strike Fighter which guarantee big jobs for a long period of time.

The people who worked in the area were ecstatic.

It is infectious once you get people involved in doing it.

Have you been able to in-source any work?

JOYCE: We were going to outsource from Georgia to Mexico the building of wiring harnesses because it's very intense touch labor. Again, it's how you look at work getting done.

The benefit the harness people had in Georgia was proximity to the final product — the C-130 — that you could never replicate in Mexico. Rather than outsource that work, we looked at whether we could engulf that work in the next higher assembly, building up the entire aircraft.

We completely redid the harness area and took 64 percent of the inventory and 15 percent of the touch labor out of the system. We are locating it right next to the aircraft and we only build one when there is a signal from the aircraft that we need one. There is a whole lot more money tied up in inventory, the boxing, the shipping, the trucking and the controls than just the 10 people working in the labor.

We told people we were going to commit to either fixing this to be lean or getting rid of it if it's not lean. If it's not lean then it is going to be cheaper to do it in Mexico. So what's our commitment? Are we going to fix it and make it lean or are we going to outsource it?

Are you reversing the trend of outsourcing manufacturing overseas?

JOYCE: Absolutely. The Japanese love to use biological analogies. The model they use is the skeleton of the fish. Everything is physically connected to the head. If you have a skeleton structure, you can build-in a reflex capability so that producers and consumers are connected by a bone. You can set up independent signaling systems about demand and consumption that are called kanban as opposed to the hunt that we were on where everything has to go through the brain with MRP-2. With kanban you create a reflex capability.

The name of the game is how many breaks in the bone can you stand? In our case we got carried away with outsourcing. We would machine a housing and then box it up and ship it across the street to get deburred. Then we'd box it back up and ship it back to the line and it would continue on. It would take four days to do a 15-second deburr. The rationalization is I'm paying skilled mechanics $15 a hour, I can get somebody to deburr for $5 an hour, so doesn't that make sense to send it out?

I can show you the ROI: it's overhead times variation times $5 versus variation times $15 and I'm going to save millions of bucks. But the support network is ignored. That's in the overhead and everybody is treated the same. So we made stupid decisions on outsourcing. The question becomes, how much of those economics can I stand?

You must have literally thousands of systems that need improvement.

JOYCE: At any one time we have 50 or 60 of these projects going.

Are we going to fix it and make it lean or are we going to outsource it?

We got carried away with outsourcing.

For instance, a project on improving the process for making the weapon's bay door on the F-22 took out three-quarters of the labor and three-quarters of the inventory.

In a machine shop in Georgia, one guy is now running the whole shop of six machines. In Skunk Works, we have an operator who works on the wing of a U-2 who was constantly getting down off the workstation to get more parts and tools and bringing them back. So we said there has to be a way that we can treat him like a surgeon, so when he says wrench, there it is.

There is a company that sells building blocks using PVC pipes that we use to build erector-set type tools that fit right around the wing of a U-2 and presents parts and tools right in front of the operator. Everything he needs is right there with him.

> *The minute you get distracted your probability of making an error has gone up dramatically.*

The design of the work is such that the operator can stay on task, stay focused on what he's doing. It's like playing golf. When you immerse yourself and keep focused, you can usually do pretty well. But the minute you get taken off task and get distracted your probability of making an error has gone up dramatically.

We need to take away all of the reasons why somebody gets distracted. It's not about intense focus. You have to concentrate in golf but you're not concentrating to the point where you're getting a headache. But you know you're concentrating almost subconsciously. That is the thing we're trying to drive here, which is to get people into the zone of comfort and take away all of the distraction. That's what we are doing in many of our projects.

Do you see the 50 or 60 percent improvements in performance reflected in your financials?

JOYCE: You can't assume those numbers are going to waltz across the bottom line. It's not going to happen. The way the score is kept is [by tallying] direct labor, support labor and materials, inventory, power plants and equipment and accounts payable. Some of this is distasteful, but to get the shareholders the payoff, then we have to talk about labor policies and overtime.

> *To get the shareholders the payoff, then we have to talk about labor policies.*

To the hourly worker, their overtime is their bonus. They get used to working a lot of hours and until you break them out of that mode and tell them they can have a life on the weekend, they almost fall into a comfort zone of coming in on Saturdays and Sundays. What if you don't have to come in on those days because you get the work done because you're more productive? That's a novel thought.

But they lose their bonus money.

JOYCE: That's what they push back on. They covet a certain level of overtime. It always comes back to a balancing act. Are you being fair to the shareholders? Are you being fair to the workforce? When you have overtime polices that have run amuck you are not being fair to the shareholders.

People get used to living on overtime money.

There is a whole aspect of lean that is built around total productive maintenance.

And maybe it's not being fair to the workers either.

JOYCE: When you get into modes where people are working seven days a week in a factory operation you have to look at the absentee rates. People make it up to themselves. They take off during the week. So you're kidding yourself.

People get used to living on overtime money. But policy decisions are exactly that. They are in there for a hard reason.

When I was at United Technologies they implemented a policy decision that no salary worker would get paid overtime. At the time, engineers and first-line supervisors were getting paid overtime, and they just came in and said no more. We're going to modify behavior. A lot of people took an instant pay cut because they were unable to dial in their own overtime and there was a lot of fretting that people were going to leave. But it didn't happen. People adjusted their lives.

In what other ways does lean change embedded behavior?

JOYCE: We started looking at why we buy capital equipment. Now we make everyone rationalize it against the big engineering flow problem, or a big system problem. If it doesn't solve a big problem, we're not going to buy it. We're not going to buy a machine that can drill twice as fast unless it makes a wing faster. But that's hard because you have people's careers built around studying faster drilling techniques.

One of the things I've learned about going on factory tours is that the companies that are best in class often have old equipment and won't replace machines that work perfectly well.

JOYCE: You can't buy your way into lean. There is a whole aspect of lean that is built around total productive maintenance. If you just take real good care of what you've got, this equipment lasts a long, long time. The question of capturing that to the bottom line is not a trivial one.

Where is Lockheed Martin now in its lean movement?

JOYCE: We've taken it in the aero sector hook, line and sinker. We are charging. The results down in our facilities are outstanding. They're just fabulous.

Obviously you start in different places on this scale. Our Fort Worth facility where we build the F-16 already had a great manufacturing discipline. They have an MRP-2 system that is the best I've ever come across. They really run it well. The challenge is to bring them to another order of magnitude in performance.

In one lean project with the F-16 forward fuselage, we took 40 percent of the inventory out and 20 percent of the labor out just by critically asking is this optimized for flow and the answer usually is no.

A really dramatic one is on the C-130 in Georgia where we looked at building a full airplane on flow principles. The standard paradigm is to build an airplane in sub areas and hoist the sections. We asked if we could build an airplane without hoisting, and you can. We're putting a line in place now where we are building a C-130 without hoisting and we're taking 30 percent of the cycle out.

Why is it better not to hoist?

JOYCE: Hoisting is waste. There is nothing in the hoist process that adds value to the product. A lot of times you hoist because of the way you configure the factory. You build the nose in once place and then you have to move it over to the assembly line. Why did you build the nose over there? Because that is the nose department. So we said why can't the nose be made right next to where it is needed on the assembly line and just slide it over on a ramp?

That's not a bad thought. Then you have line of sight between the producer of the nose and the needer of the nose and you can put up a signaling system and kill the MRP contact between them.

There are even multiplying effects which make hoisting disastrously pure waste because when you hoist something overhead, all work below has to stop for safety reasons and constraints. If you're hoisting over a long part of the shop, the totality of the shop takes a break.

Did your shop floor people have a lot to do with this change? Was it something they had been thinking of for a long time?

JOYCE: The part I don't buy into is the idea that you can just go out to the operators and they'll tell you what you need to do. When you get stuck that is when you want to bring people who are doing it together and tell them that within the bounds of flow, we have these things we have to solve, let's get together and solve them. You have to give them the knowledge of what it is you're trying to make happen.

Every puzzle is easy once you see the answer but when you don't know the answer and all you have is the puzzle it takes some really creative thinking to break the code. That is where operators are good because they have been touching it for so long. Putting them on the team that says, "Here is the puzzle, here are the constraints to the puzzle; it's not random ideas we're throwing out; here is what I need your help with; and oh, by the way, if you think moving this piece of equipment is going to do it better, then it will be moved." And when they show up and it's in a new position and it was their idea, they're hooked.

How does Six Sigma quality fit into the lean equation?

JOYCE: There are all kinds of tools to tap into to get friction out of the system. Six Sigma is one. We had a meeting with GE and their business executives in the engines group and they're on this Six-Sigma kick from [AlliedSignal CEO Larry] Bossidy talking to [former GE chairman Jack] Welch. I feel they have the cart before the horse.

I'll give you an example. We went into an area where we build extrusions that become frame assemblies that go into the C-130. It was a batch-

Why can't the nose be made right next to where it is needed on the assembly line?

Six Sigma is a tool to get friction out of the system.

Don't jump into the quality loop first because if you do you can generate a lot of waste.

Single-piece flow is intolerant of error.

and-queue factory with scheduling systems, and we said we've got to make this conform to the rules of lean.

Here is the puzzle. There were 6,000 part numbers and 1,300 routings, all small volume. Show me how you are going to do one-piece flow with that mess. We put the team together, they studied it and analyzed it and came up with the answer of standardizing to five part families and 25 routings.

In that process there were nine ways to deburr the edges off the parts, all of which were available somewhere in the factory. We can't stand that. Let's standardize on one way to deburr all the parts.

So we analyzed it and we came up with one. Now we have people engaged in having ownership in selecting the one. It's at that point that we Six Sigma the one that we've chosen. Let's make sure that one deburr humms, that it never breaks down.

That is opposed to going out and applying Six Sigma to nine processes that deburr parts. Why would you want to do that? Because Six Sigma is the thing to do. Quality is where it's at. Yeah, in its time. In its place.

You have to define the system first and then make it work. Don't jump into the quality loop first because if you do you can generate a lot of waste.

What are some of most difficult aspects of implementing a lean manufacturing system?

JOYCE: Invariably you're going to run into problems almost immediately because the one thing about lean and single-piece flow is that it is intolerant of error. Everything that is said and written about the Saturn plant that describes how everyone is empowered to shut down the line is bunk. If you're really doing single-piece flow and you run into a problem, the whole system shuts itself down. You don't have to pull anything. It stops. Now wanting to signal to people that you have trouble, that is where signaling systems are very valuable.

Once we get the line up and running is when Deming and Six Sigma and all of that TQM stuff is absolutely required. If you have a problem, then you determine, like Deming said, if it is a special-cause or common-cause problem. People look at you like you have two heads and wonder what you're talking about when you ask them this question. But not all problems should be solved the same way. Special-cause problems just creep in and are not systemic. You can usually mistake proof those out. If you put a part in backwards, then stick this pin in there and it can't go in backwards any more. Done, problem solved.

Then there are the common-cause problems, meaning they are embedded in the system design. For instance, if I weld something and the weld process only has a 90 percent yield because chemistry and heat, you might need a statistical process control in there to let you know when something is going astray.

There is a whole toolset under Six Sigma of all different kinds of SPC techniques that you can dial into the particular one you need. Maybe this one needs a control chart. Okay, what kind of control chart?

Structured problem solving has its place, and guess what? In single-piece flow you can't live without it. So you better know what you're talking about.

The same is true with machine maintenance. In the old model, if the machine breaks down, you use another machine. Now when you're doing single-piece flow and you've got one machine and it goes down and you're not making anything today or tomorrow, all of a sudden making sure that machine doesn't go down takes on new significance. That stress level forces you to do maintenance.

What role does information technology play in the lean manufacturing model?

JOYCE: There is a school of thought that if I do this well, if I get the skeleton structure and get the reflex capability and don't have to have everything go back to the brain, how much IT do I need?

How much IT do I need?

When we start working with some of these cells making simple parts, it's very typical that we have anywhere between 25 and 30 places where we have to go back to the information management system for material transactions. That's not even mentioning financial transactions or people transactions just for material. When we go and lean it we can take the 30 down to two. But there are still two. And two, times two, times two becomes a very large complex system.

Is there a place for IT? I'm squarely on the side that says absolutely yes, the question is how.

There is a camp that says absolutely not. I was at a conference not long ago and somebody who is really into this in another industry was asked what he does when the SAPs of the world come knocking at the door, and he said, "It's simple, I send them to my competition because they're going to bleed money off of them and distract them from what they really should be doing."

One concern is it's taking the best and the brightest to stand up an information system to track 23 information check points for every part number instead of taking the same resource pool that says give me a system that only has two.

Somehow lean and ERP have to play together.

But somehow the two have to play together.

If you look at building a C-130 aircraft, what is the best way to use all of the things we have at our disposal to control material movement through this very complex system of parts? It's a combination of MRP thinking and lean thinking.

I've studied the hell out of Toyota's material planning system and what you need to do is build in flexibilities. To build an airplane as complex as this, we have to define relationships between supply sources and consumers. What is the planning methodology? What is the disbursement trigger? How do we get inventory under control? What is the right con-

The nice thing about kanban is it deals with variation before the fact.

Kanban allows a degree of variation.

trol mechanism that exists between the consumer and producer?

If you go to the next level of kanban loops, you have a reflex capability tool that is more applicable. What a kanban [signal card] loop does is set up a relational loop between a producer and a consumer. The nice thing about kanban is it deals with variation before the fact. The problem with MRP systems is they always try to get to perfection and they deal with variation after the fact. If you have to build one [component] it tells you all the parts and requirements backed up by a lead time and then, boom, go. After that, all the variation comes in. There are drawing changes, quality problems and people not showing up.

You are either on the plan or off the plan. Every two weeks they try to come back and rebaseline the plan to account for all the variation that occurred. The downside is it creates a lot of transactional traffic and by the time you're down at the value stream, you're getting whipsawed: push that requirement out, pull that one in, push it out, pull it in. So you have hundreds of people online daily moving stuff out and moving stuff back in to accommodate the perfect schedule. Hence the analogy that it's like playing sports in a full-body cast. You have no flexibility, you're locked in.

Kanban allows you to set up a relational loop between a producer and a consumer of a recurring item and build in variation before the fact. The error of the MRP system is usually measured inventory: the inventory is not capped, so people can push out and pull in things.

In the kanban world, you set up a relationship between a producer and a consumer that says, "I have to give you roughly five of these parts per week, let's deal with variation beforehand and say we'll allow seven parts to exist in the loop between you and me but I'm not going to send you one until you signal and only at that time will I send it to you. We'll also set a limit that there are only seven times you'll signal me in the loop. So between us we'll allow a cap of inventory.

"As variation comes in so long as we don't violate the relationship set between us we do nothing. If you need six parts instead of five, that's okay because we have a loop for seven and we do nothing. If you don't need five but four, then there is no reason to do anything. But if you don't need five but one, then maybe we should change the relationship."

Kanban allows that degree of variation inside of it, so that as long as the variation stays within the band, you're okay and don't have to do anything and you take all this transactional junk out of the information management system.

Does Lockheed Martin's SAP implementation fit this model?
JOYCE: When you go through the entire F-22 and start talking about the participation of other plants, internal lean cells that make products, independent requirements such as spares and outside suppliers, then you have all these relational databases that you not only have to define but manage.

I look at the ERP world and say why can't I embed that in my information launch so that when I lay this out it tells me that we have to put five kanbans between me and you and we'll do okay. A lot of that is done manually today, but an ERP system can do that for you.

We've quizzed SAP on what they've got and the building blocks to do that are in their system, you just have to configure it. So we can embed all of the logic for doing it right in the information management system. Let's go do that because it's powerful in that it uses a whole lot less resources than I'm using today to do that same job.

Is it hard to do?
JOYCE: I've become a fan of the ERP system because right now there is nothing else out there that can do it. We've got maps laid out for every product we make. I can't imagine sitting here 10 years from now not having done anything with the information revolution only because I'm deathly afraid that one of my competitors will. It's such a bold undertaking that the only part I get suspicious about is the SAPs of the world have done a great job of packaging the thing. They've written the rules of engagement and they're masters at it.

We already have things going on in our Fort Worth facility that pick up on information management without ERP. It's similar to the Wal-Mart model. We have bar-code scanning systems set up on the factory floor tied to a long-term agreement with Grainger where for all non-product consumable materials from Q-tip swabs to gloves we use in the factory, we have hand-held bar code readers with antennas on them and antennas on the roof and we bar-code scan everything with a computer screen that asks you questions.

As soon as we consume, Grainger gets it and they come in three times a day and replenish. It fits into the lean model perfectly. By going this way, we killed five ordering and receiving processes. We threw out all of the paperwork transfers.

Now you have to work through every issue as it comes up because even with Grainger we had negotiations with the union where they didn't want suppliers to walk right out on the floor and put it in their work area. So the supplier takes it as far as they can and somebody picks it up. We're willing to give a little bit to get a little bit. Ultimately, you'd love for the supplier to come in and manage the shelf for you and we can get there ultimately. In the balance of everything you have to keep people happy and you have to flex with it.

Are you requiring that your suppliers adopt lean systems?
JOYCE: We sent every supplier a letter and a copy of Womack's book that said here is where we are going guys, you better get on board.

Are you going to assess their abilities?
JOYCE: We're kicking off what we're calling a lean supply chain with each one of our tier-one suppliers. We've already been to Rolls Royce and

I've become a fan of the ERP system.

Ultimately, you'd love for the supplier to come in and manage the shelf for you.

We'll physically track how our product gets made in their facility.

Sanders. We've made a commitment that says we want to lean-out making the product, information and solving technical problems. We need to change the way we play the game.

We've told them the new rules. We're going to assign to them experts who know lean flow; someone who has change authority for product; someone who understands information management; someone associated with scheduling; and someone who understands quality requirements. We want our suppliers to have a team of counterparts.

Then we are going to have a joint executive sponsor, our vice president for the program and the president of their company who will review the results every two months. We're going to have a quarterly report out to our own CEO.

We'll physically track how our product gets made in their facility and fix it and then commit to jointly working our waste.

JANNEY MONTGOMERY SCOTT LLC

There aren't many financial analysts who base their stock recommendations on whether a company has adopted lean manufacturing techniques. But there is at least one who judges the investment prospects of a company by taking a factory tour to determine whether a company's stock is worth purchasing.

Cliff Ransom, director of research at Janney Montgomery Scott LLC, the Philadelphia-based investment firm founded in 1933, spends his days researching traditional manufacturing companies. He has found that 90 percent of them have no knowledge of basic lean principles such as muda, takt time and 5-S. "Maybe 5 percent of them are bonafide practitioners of this fine art and it's maybe one, two or three percent that really get it," he explains.

It's not necessary for a company to embrace lean per se, he insists. But it must use a production system that incorporates its basic tenets. "There are lots of ways to get to heaven," Ransom notes. "It can be ITW's 80/20 process. It can be the Danaher Business System, or Six Sigma, demand flow or lean sigma. They have their roots in the same thing: elimination of variability and the elimination of waste." Ransom was working at State Street Research when he conducted this interview.

The creme de la creme of Wall Street don't get it.

Why are there so few financial analysts following companies based upon their lean practices?

RANSOM: In my business, it takes a very long time to change investor attitudes so that it is reflected in the multiple. We can argue that it took GE 20 years of working on this and they've only had a superior multiple for the last 10 years. Danaher has been at it for 10 or 11 years and they only got a superior multiple in the last three or four. ITW has been doing it for 25 years.

Despite their success with lean production, most people have never heard of Danaher or ITW.

RANSOM: Danaher has been invaluable to me as an investor, as an analyst and as a businessman and I was exposed early to their learning process and they've been a benchmark for me. I'm the only guy on the buy side who has done the full Danaher Business System training class. I'm the only guy who's ever done a kaizen with Shingijutsu. I'm the only guy who's ever done a kaizen with TBM. So I know enough about it to be dangerous.

Danaher did a one-day primer on lean for about 20 stock market analysts at their Pacific Scientific Division in Massachusetts. These are the brightest of bright on Wall Street who were there because they wanted to learn about lean. They had just gone through a whole day of training...and they did not have a clue as to what lean was about.

When the crowd broke up, I told my partner that this was the full employment syndrome at work. We had an indisputable competitive edge because these guys — the creme de la creme of Wall Street — don't get it and they're not going to get it.

So there isn't any pressure from Wall Street for industrial companies to adopt lean?

RANSOM: People tell me that they're doing it and I walk into their

You go into these plants and the lights aren't good.

factories and I just see too many big things that are wrong. You just walk in and start counting. I have been having a running war with Caterpillar. I've been in nine or 10 of their plants and I have said you have been asleep at the switch since the late 1980s and early 1990s. You go into these plants and the lights aren't good. If you have bolsters around the machines to keep the oil from coming out, it's wrong. If you even have absorbent material in your store room, it's wrong, you're not world class. You shouldn't have to buy it.

They look at me as if I have two heads. I ask, "Where are the visual aides? Where are the dashboards? Where is it posted in a cell? Where is takt time? Tell me what your takt time is?" They don't know.

So I say well that's fine, I'm not going to give them one or two or three or five more multiple points because it all speaks to consistency and sustainability which is what multiples are all about.

What it means is you make good investments for your clients, which at the end of the day is my mission.

Have you seen recent examples of companies adopting lean successfully?

RANSOM: In the last six or seven years, JLG Industries, which invented and still dominates the aerial work platform market, has had a home-grown system. Teleflex, which is a wonderful $2-billion a year company, is now on its 25th or 26th consecutive year of straight up revenues which go straight to EPS. It's a marvelous corporate record. They undertook a derivative of the Toyota Production System.

Danaher dates from 1988 and 1989. Allied Sigma and their whole Six Sigma effort dates from 1990. The Six Sigma effort at Black & Decker is only five or six years old.

People are now saying Six Sigma is a fad not worth pursuing. This was expressed in an article in [the January 22, 2001 edition of] Fortune [entitled "Why You Can Safely Ignore Six Sigma"] saying that Six Sigma has no payoff for investors.

RANSOM: Let me tell you something, they're just dead wrong. First of all, it means they don't understand Six Sigma. You know, GE said a couple of things over the last six years. They said they are going to globalize. They're going to drive into service businesses. They're going to adopt Six Sigma and digitize the whole firm. And in doing so, they took one of the largest corporations in the world and they accelerated their growth rate. They expanded their already high margins.

There is a reason GE carries a premium multiple.

There is a reason why GE carries a premium multiple and it's because there is that kind of consistency and that is what it's all about. Globalization, services, Six Sigma, digitization, and they've added a fifth thing, which is they're going to be a learning company — challenge everything all the time. Their core competency is not manufacturing or service but the global recruiting and nurturing of the world's best people and the cultivation of an insatiable desire to learn and to stretch and do things better every day.

It sounds like continuous improvement to me.
RANSOM: Absolutely. Absolutely. There is a reason why Danaher and UTX carry premium multiples. Even with earnings being whacked around with auto and construction, there is a reason why ITW still sells at a fairly rich multiple. Anybody who doesn't believe that is doomed to an average or sub-par multiple. If you can't prove it, you're not going to get it. Maybe Fortune says that because there are only five or 10 companies that get that premium; but I don't have to own more than three of them in my business. I just have to pick the right three out of 10.

There aren't too many of those stocks, are there?
RANSOM: There is a very limited number. Everybody has some jargon, but you have to practice what you preach. That is why I go visit factories because I learn, for instance, that when all of my colleagues think that Caterpillar is a very efficient manufacturing company I know that it simply isn't.

So visiting a factory is one of the best things an analyst can do?
RANSOM: Absolutely. You see the minute you walk into the door whether or not they are living by the fancy vision statement at the front of their annual report. It doesn't matter what they have on the walls on the headquarters offices. It matters what they have on the walls of the factory. And if you see inventory stacked up at every stage of production and if you see inventory racks 30 feet high stretching for 10 football fields, you know they're not doing it right.

I walked into an Omniquip factory with a broker from Bear Stearns. I looked in the door of the factory and I said we can leave now. He said, "What do you mean?" I said, "I see five or six major errors that they're doing right now and we don't need to be here. We can go to the next appointment." And he said, "Come on Cliff, these guys have been waiting for us for six weeks and they're all set up."

So we walked through the factory and in about an hour and a half, I filled out two pages of things that were not little errors: routing; material flow; the paint room in one corner and everything else in the other corner; testing done at the end of the line instead of in the line. It was all stuff that I thought was basic.

I don't mind when a factory stinks if the factory knows it stinks and they tell me that they understand that it's a half-full glass and not a half-empty glass. [Omniquip] thought they were the cat's pajamas and of course they wound up getting in trouble and they put themselves up for sale and two of their competitors in related lines of business — JLG and Terex —were trying to figure out who should bid $11 and who should bid $11.50 a share. Then Textron came in at the eleventh hour and paid $20.

You see the minute you walk into the door whether or not they are living by the fancy vision statement at the front of their annual report.

Textron bought it and it's been a nightmare ever since. I said to Lew Campbell, the chairman, "I don't mind that you made a mistake but I'm not going to buy your stock until you admit your mistake." It's like the old line about bank loan officers: Unless you have a few loans go belly up you're not a good loan officer. Every once in a while you buy something that doesn't work, but don't keep telling me that it was a great buy. Omniquip continues to lose share and I had that insight way into the process.

Well a cynic would have said if you bought the stock at $10 it would have gotten bought out at $21 and I say if I had inside information I could go to prison if I use it and, secondly, it's a hard way other than say 5 percent of your decision process to think there is a greater fool, or a "strategic buyer."

The companies that understand lean are long-term buys, aren't they, because it takes a long time to implement?

RANSOM: I think ITW made 50 acquisitions last year. They know how to buy companies and integrate them. This came home to me first when I really understood the power of the Danaher Business System as an acquisition and integration tool.

When Lou Horvath who ran the Teleflex Production System [first arrived] they had an extraordinarily successful record that was created along decentralized lines. Plant managers were very close to their customers, very independent and very decentralized. He said that these guys didn't want him to come in and tell them that their typical long transfer lines were the wrong way to do it. Instead, he said, "We're going to go here in the corner and we're going to take one little piece of your business and we're going to move some equipment around and train some people and then you tell me whether you like it. Just try it."

They did one little cell and these guys were all good businessmen and then they changed their compensation plans to return on invested capital, return on capital employed, inventory turns and service standards and then they said, "Wow, this stuff works." That's when they embraced it. That is when it gets exciting.

Boeing is a great example. They spent 10 years looking at this stuff. They had people going to Japan in the late '80s, but they had 200,000-plus employees and they were all engineers and the mantra of the company was higher, faster, further. They had 85 percent of the installed base and they didn't understand that inventory turns of two were not acceptable. They began to push harder on this and Debbie Hopkins came in and she was a big boost and then Allen Mulally who took over the Boeing Commercial Airplane Group said this is how we're going to run the business. Now they're generating four and five billion dollars a year in cash. It's coming from a lot of things, but a lot of the things it's coming from is working capital.

They changed their compensation plans to return on invested capital, return on capital employed, inventory turns and service standards.

What happens to companies that haven't adopted lean?

RANSOM: The good guys are going to be generating cash and buying stuff like mad. UTX has a very deep pipeline. Danaher has a very deep pipeline. Roper has a very deep pipeline. The guys who wouldn't talk to them two years ago have to talk to them now.

Does an economic downturn spark an interest in lean?

RANSOM: No. I've been looking at this only for 10 years and I'm amazed how slowly this has spread across industry. It has spread into and through specific companies and sometimes even just specific divisions, but it hasn't spread to their competitors or other kinds of industries and I keep asking, "Don't they read the literature? Don't they look at the financial statements, the stock performance, the price/earnings multiples of the companies that do it right? Why wouldn't that be a great motivator?" I'm always amazed at the absence of the adoptability.

Is it because it's viewed as another trend, especially since there have been so many lately, such as TQM, reengineering, re-reengineering, agile manufacturing and the B2B trade exchanges?

RANSOM: There are a great many people who think lean is a fad and they are going to get their lunch eaten by people who know better. We can argue about Deming and TQM and quality circles, but that stuff helped all those companies. Don't kid yourself, the guys who are good Deming devotees and who were good TQM advocates and who did quality circles the right way 15 or 20 years ago, those companies got better. With what lean does to floor space and to inventory, some of these companies will never build bricks and mortar again.

I went through a Paccar plant making a big class-A truck — a big assembly job — and they had a chain-pull assembly line. I've been taught that that is a bad thing to have because it's inflexible and I was getting ready to be pissed off and then I started watching this stuff coming in and they were building 50 trucks a day and there were seven chassis in the yard because they are going into the line and they had WIP turns in that plant of 42 times and there is nothing wrong with that plant. If you can't get WIP once a week, you're doing something wrong.

Do you have any examples of companies that adopted lean and got it wrong or just did not have the patience to implement it?

RANSOM: I worried a little bit that it happened at Stanley Works because so many people left and they began to move a lot of production offshore. By my interpretation, they began to feel that rather than fight the war domestically, they would fight the war with a cost base overseas. The TBM guys have a fit when I talk about outsourcing because I say that unless it's a commodity, don't outsource. But the fact of the matter is margins are rising at Stanley Works so they have to be doing something right.

I'm amazed how slowly this has spread across industry.

If you can't get WIP once a week, you're doing something wrong.

Once you start having success, you don't get many examples of where it fails.

The validity of the new economy has become hogwash...

Is it a good sign if a company hires Shingijutsu?

RANSOM: It's a good sign because Shingijutsu won't take the assignment unless they think they can make it work. I was frankly amazed that they went to Stanley Works. It precipitated a minor crisis with Danaher because Danaher is a direct competitor.

From an investor's point of view, what are the difficulties companies face in adopting a lean business model?

RANSOM: A lot of upper- to middle-level floor supervisors have a very hard time with empowerment and participatory management. "Oh my God, you're going to ask workers to act independently and let them stop the line?" There are emotional problems.

But once you start having success, you don't get many examples of where it fails. You get examples of where it atrophies or you do a kaizen and you think you fixed it and they forget that kaizen means good change, which is a continuous improvement process that never ends. I've been in cells that have been kaizened eight and 10 times and every time you attack them you get benefits.

Danaher isn't a very well known company yet is always mentioned as being perhaps the best example of a lean enterprise.

RANSOM: They only care about their shareholders and their customers. They don't even talk to the Wall Street Journal. They don't want to give every executive headhunter in America a roadmap of who they can steal. They didn't speak with James Womack [president of the Lean Enterprise Institute and author of *Lean Thinking*]. Yet if there are nine case studies in that book, five of them are based on the work of Danaher alumni and four of those were people who basically failed at Danaher. But they learned so much they were able to go and transform other companies. Now does that tell you about the power of the process?

Would the creation of a lean portfolio fund be a good opportunity?

RANSOM: Here's the problem. You can have all the knowledge in the world and still be wrong on your stock picks because the market can get negative. There was nothing wrong with the earnings of these companies in 1998, but absolutely not one new dollar of incremental investment went to them. During 1998, it was awful. My performance looked like '72, '73 and '74. You have to remember that being right does not necessarily mean you've enriched your client. You always have to remember where the market is.

Since the middle of 1999 and certainly since March 10 of 2000 — it's funny how those dates stick in your head — the validity of the new economy has become hogwash...There is nothing new under the sun. There are new tools for the real economy. If you can't generate cash, you're out of business. At one time Amazon was putting a check for $4.36 in every book they mailed out. That just doesn't work.

The companies that differentiate themselves will be rewarded in the stock market.

In the meantime, Danaher, UTX, Teleflex and Roper Industries are all selling near their all time highs, thank God.

My theory is — and it's been true since GE went to a 40 multiple and Danaher and Tyco went to a 30 multiple — that the companies that differentiate themselves will be rewarded in the stock market and the relative performance of those companies against the market has been phenomenal.

WIREMOLD CO.

Wiremold is a rare company. It has achieved national and international prominence not so much for the products it makes, but for the manner in which it makes them. Under the 10-year stewardship of Art Byrne, the company was one of the first in the United States to embrace the production and management techniques espoused by the creators of the Toyota Production System.

Byrne comes out of a small cadre of people trained in lean principles while at Danaher Corp. in the late 1980s. When he joined Wiremold in 1991, the company was a small, Hartford-based maker of wire and cable management systems for buildings. Byrne brought his team of consultants with him from Shingijutsu, men who perfected the Toyota Production System, and he went to work at turning around a company that had no cash, low profits, declining market share and poor customer service.

Since then, the lean system he introduced has sparked a turnaround with results that most manufacturing firms would envy. The company's sales have grown by more than a factor of four to $460 million, or by more than 38 percent per year. Its operating margin exceeds 12 percent. It continues to double inventory turns every two years and has improved quality by at least a factor of 10. The company offers 35,000 products, each of which it is capable of producing every day.

You can't look at it as a manufacturing thing.

Start it as a business philosophy.

What advice do you have for companies that are considering adopting a lean manufacturing strategy?

BYRNE: You can't look at it as a manufacturing thing. Companies that look at lean as a manufacturing exercise can't do it. Most companies say lean and then put the word manufacturing after it. They get the manufacturing guy to go to a workshop to see if there is anything there for them. When you approach it that way, you can get some benefit, but it's not what you're going to get when you adopt it as a business strategy.

People call us all the time wanting to come here to see what we're doing. Over the years we've seen a lot of different companies and people start this, and mostly they fail. The bigger companies fail at this quite badly because their emphasis and strategies are somewhere else. I've watched companies create a manager for lean and a separate guy for total quality, and all they do is get themselves and the whole organization very confused.

We've seen cases where a company says we want to do lean and we need someone to come help. Someone tells them what they need to do and they say, "Oh, we didn't think we needed to do all those things, so we'll pick one aspect from over here and one from over there."

Is the place to start a lean implementation in the production area of a company?

BYRNE: You have to start it as a business philosophy. If you don't look at it as a business philosophy and as an approach for the way you're going to run your overall business and how you're going to beat your competition, then you're going to suboptimize anything you're going to do.

How about companies that try to adopt lean by implementing just-in-time production practices?

BYRNE: There is always another word after just-in-time, which is usually just-in-time inventory. The concept is you take it to most of your suppliers and beat the heck out of them. The automotive companies are famous for this. It never became a business philosophy.

Lean is the same way. It has gotten the word manufacturing stuck in after it so people think, "Lean manufacturing, oh, that's something we can delegate down to the manufacturing guys."

JIT never became a business philosophy.

Yet if you do that, what you find is that nobody told the sales and marketing guys what this was all about. They're off doing things that are anti-lean. They're doing things that make it eight or 10 times harder to do anything resembling lean. They're putting in massive sales promotions; they're doing end-of-the-month deals; they're trying to load up the distributor. All of these behaviors are anti what you're trying to do in the factory.

What is the most common cause of failure among companies trying to implement lean?

BYRNE: We've watched a lot of companies fail because lean doesn't seem to apply to accounting. Some of the toughest barriers are the accounting and the computer systems that are set up for batch or standard cost. We get a lot of people who come here and say, "Can you have your finance guy come and talk to our finance guys because we've been doing lean for quite a few months now, but our finance guys are killing us. They still want the old measurements. They want to look at things the old way. They're not giving us the data that we need and we're all just confused."

Most company presidents and CEOs are not comfortable in their factories.

You make it so much harder for yourself if you think of lean as a factory thing. Most company presidents and CEOs are not comfortable in their factories. They come out of finance or marketing and so manufacturing is just something that should happen. They often have a manufacturing guy who says, "Just leave it to me and I'll take care of it." This is the way most manufacturing guys behave, but trying to get the entire organization to change is difficult.

How important is it to have buy-in from the CEO?

BYRNE: The advice we give to anyone who talks to us is if you can't get the CEO to lead this, then don't start because you're just wasting your time. You're going to get more confused. You're going to give the whole idea a bad name. You're not going to be successful and you're going to make it impossible for someone to come along later and do it because everyone in the organization will say, "Oh, we tried that and it failed." It failed because you set it up to fail.

If you can't get the CEO to lead this, don't start.

This is a major, strategic, cultural change. If you go to Toyota you hardly ever find senior executives who haven't at some point during their career spent a couple of years on the shop floor doing kaizen. The culture in their company demands that. If you don't know how to do it and if you don't know what it's all about, you're not going to be successful in that company.

More companies are outsourcing their production or moving it to Mexico or China. Is that a good way to reduce costs and stay competitive?

BYRNE: You really confuse people when you have a major thrust in outsourcing and you've got another major thrust of doing lean. You can almost guarantee that when a company has that dual thrust, the real thrust is to move everything to Mexico, because lean is a much harder thing to do than move everything to Mexico. The organization will take the easier route all the time.

On a piece of paper you can say, "Wow, if I move to Mexico, I'll have the same number of people and they cost 75 percent less. Man, look at how much money I can save. Let's go."

No one thinks about how long you're making the supply chain or how much inventory you're going to put in the system, or how difficult it is to get back into stock when you're out, or any of the other potential problems and the costs associated with those problems. It's hard to quantify those costs. It's easy to say, "I have 100 people in Indiana who cost $20 an hour and if I have the same 100 people in Juarez and they cost me $3 an hour, shizam, let's go."

Is there a temptation for Wiremold to move production to a place where you pay people $1.25 an hour, and potentially really whip your competition?

BYRNE: We don't have that temptation at all, although we have a factory in China that is a very good lean factory and a lean factory in China is almost an oxymoron. People go there and they have three times the number of people they have somewhere else and think nothing of it because the labor costs are so cheap. We went there to sell product into China.

Is there any way to make a lean implementation easier than it is?

BYRNE: You have to think of companies as nothing but a collection of people. My collection of people competes against your collection of people to service the same customer. If you want to go lean, how are you going to do that? What you need is knowledge.

We can tell you all the principles in about 20 minutes. They're all simple. They make perfect sense. If that's the case, why don't I just tell my guys, "Look here are the two pages of principles, go do this." Why can't they do that? What's so hard?

It's a people issue. That's why it's hard. Getting people to change — to do things differently than they have done them — is really, really hard.

You can give them the principles and say we're going to change, but what happens is you get down the path a little way and you have a bunch

Lean is much harder to do than move everything to Mexico.

It's a people issue. That's why it's hard.

of guys in a meeting and they're all excited and then one guy says what happens when this occurs? Oops, we don't know how to solve that, so let's just go back to what we know and what we know is batch or some form of batch.

The key for a company that has no knowledge but has a CEO who wants to do it is obtaining the knowledge. That is the key. How do I obtain the knowledge of how to start this? Where do we start? How do we organize? You have to have the knowledge that pushes you through the barrier of being in that meeting when nine out of 10 guys say you can't do that, it will never work.

Are the successes achieved by Wiremold or Toyota enough to motivate more companies to adopt a lean system?
BYRNE: As a general rule, no, not at all.

Why?
BYRNE: In lots of discussions with CEOs over the years you say, "Here is a list of what is possible." It's a list that should knock their socks off, and you say: "By the way, it's not capital intensive at all. There is no capital involved and you can get these gains."

People don't believe it. They say it's not possible — that those gains are too big. If they do believe that you did it, then they say, "I can understand how you did it, but you're different from us. We're bigger or we're smaller or we're in a different industry, or we have plants in other countries, or you can't transport this overseas, or what if it fails?"

I've heard all the excuses.

Companies don't do it in general because they say they're doing just fine. They don't see any pressure. They have good customer service. They say, "Well we only turn inventory three times, but everyone in my industry does the same thing and I need to do that to supply the customer and even with the three turns I have some customer service issues once in a while but I'm making good margin. I'm growing, I have a little market share, why should I want to go do this other thing?"

These are very traditional batch and queue operations that invest like crazy in automation. That's a very capital intensive go-gain-market-share kind of approach. They are very willing to invest in big automation on a forecast before they even know they're going to have a market or not. It's the opposite approach to the one we take.

How important is it for you to have an outside consultant involved in the implementation?
BYRNE: Let's go back to the example of the CEO who wants to do it but he has nobody in his company who knows how. How do you break that barrier? Well, you need outside consultants to show you how to organize the approach; how to go about it; how to set up a program and then come work with you on a regular basis. What they're doing is train-

I've heard all the excuses.

ing your people how to think differently. Without the outside consultant it's just about impossible to do this.

You might be able to hire someone from outside your company who has done it someplace else. The problem is you have to be careful with that because there isn't a manufacturing guy out there who doesn't have a resume that says he is a lean expert — a Mr. Just-In-Time who has done it all. We see those resumes all the time and most of them are nonsense because there aren't many companies doing this. What you have are guys who know some buzzwords, but are basically batch guys.

There are very few guys in the United States who can really do this type of consulting work. The network of most of the people doing this has grown out of a very small group from Danaher. If you look at companies that are successfully doing this, you'll find a Danaher connection to it and some Shingijutsu connection to it.

Are you still using Shingijutsu at Wiremold?
BYRNE: Absolutely. And they're still teaching us stuff. I have people who say we can cut back now because we know how to do it. And I say no way. The day I let them out of here or let off the consulting pressure I'm putting on people is the day I start going backwards.

There is no easy or fast way to implement a lean business system, is there?
BYRNE: This is a physical thing. You can't just reprogram your computer system and, baboom, off you go. That was the promise of MRP. It never worked. It's a lazy man's way of doing it.

This is physical. You're going to have to move every machine in the factory maybe six or eight times. When you say that, you get the: "Oh, gee, we don't want to do that because we haven't moved any of these machines for 20 years. You want to move them six or eight times over the next three years?"

"Yes."

"Well how do you know that?"

"Experience."

"Oh, that sounds like it's going to take a lot of effort and maybe we shouldn't start down that path. Couldn't we do something else?"

Let's talk about setup for a second because it helps to answer your question.

Say you ran a company and it takes three hours to changeover and you came and spent a day with us and you went home, got all of your setup guys in a room and told them: "I've seen it. This is it. It has taken us three hours to change over for the last 25 years and as of now, I need you all to change over in less than five minutes."

These guys have been running their machines for you for 20 years and you come in and tell them this revelation. What do you think they're going to say to you?

There are very few guys in the United States who can really do lean consulting work.

This is physical.

They're going to tell you why you can't do it.

First of all they'll think you're nuts. They'll say: "Haven't you learned anything in all these years you've been here? You know it takes this long."

When they find out that you're really kind of serious, now you're going to get The List. This is the list of why it can't be done. And you know what? It will be a pretty good list. It will make a lot of sense. Unless you're good at this, unless you know how specifically to do this and to show them how to do this, it's impossible for you to overcome the list because the list comes out of the guys who do this every day. They're going to tell you why you can't do it. So are you stumped?

This is why people fail. They're stumped.

What are you going to do when they give you The List? How are you going to show them? You can't just tell them, you just tried that and it didn't work. So now you're forced to show them that this can happen. You're forced to make them understand what is possible.

When I arrived at Wiremold, we had 1,600 different dies and we had to get them all to the same shut height. What do you think people said when I said let's do that? They said, "But there are 1,600 dies. Do you realize what a project that is going to be?" I said, "Yeah. If we don't get started now we probably won't ever get there. So let's start with the ones we use the most and go from there." We had people working full time doing nothing but converting dies to the same height for three or four years.

Wiremold is now 10 years into the process. Have the barriers changed over time?

BYRNE: The fundamental barriers are always the sam, but sometimes the next barrier is harder than the first barrier. Putting in a really well functioning kanban system was a harder barrier than getting from three-hour setups down to two-minute setups. Getting the kanban system to work smoothly was a harder barrier than moving into one-piece flow cells. That stuff is pretty easy.

You have to switch from MRP to using kanban cards.

As you get to new levels, some of those barriers don't seem like they should be harder, but they are because you have to have a discipline across every aspect of the company. You have to switch from making things on an MRP system to making all of your products using kanban cards. To replenish something can create three or four or five — maybe even six — additional layers of kanban cards. To get people to understand that and try to implement that takes a lot of time.

The main barrier is always the same. It's always people. It's not a technology thing at all. This is technology simple. We don't make a lot of capital investments.

How do you get people to take the next step? How do you get them to understand that there are another 20 steps after that?

BYRNE: The difficulty might be Western economies in general and the difference between Christian and Eastern religions. We believe in an absolute — a beginning and end. You die, that's it. In Asia, you can come back as a cat, a dog or a prince. You can come back a lot of times. So there is never an absolute ending.

We translate that into, "I did a kaizen, this is the most perfect way to do it, period. Never go back and look at it again." That's a problem. The Japanese will go back and look at something 40 or 50 times. We've kaizened every part of our business — every cell, every process — multiple times. You just have to keep going back. We are never going to stop. The crazy thing is that maybe the first time through you get a 50 percent productivity gain, the next time through you're going to get 100 percent. That is a mindboggling thing for people to think about.

We are never going to stop.

Do you see the same results the eighth time through?
BYRNE: Yes. With one of our initial cells, we went from eight people down to four, a 50 percent productivity gain. Then we went from four to two, same thing. Then we went from two to one. The percentage gain was much bigger.

Can you go from one to none?
BYRNE: You effectively do that by incorporating other things into their jobs. One person is now doing two or three other rows of tasks.

Do they rebel against having to do so much more?
BYRNE: The amazing thing here is that the main people barrier isn't the people on the shop floor doing the work, it's the middle management. The managers fight this more than your shop floor people because it's a bigger threat to them. If you spent the last 25 years putting in a manufacturing system for your company and I show up, take a plant tour and we come back into the office and I say, "Look, I've seen it and it's all no good." What's your reaction to that? "Hey, I've been doing this for 25 years, who are you to come in here and tell me that? You don't know my business; you don't know my industry; you don't know anything and I've been told for 25 years that I've been doing a great job. I've been promoted. I've gotten raises."

The main barrier is middle management.

Your tendency is to fight me. The number of people who would take the approach of saying, "Oh, really, you think so, can you show me how to make it better?" — as opposed to, "Screw you." — is very, very small. Less than 5 percent of the people say, okay, show me. Most people are defensive, so you have to get over that.

I have seen so many organizations where the CEO gets enlightened. He wants to do it and someone tells him he has to have outside consultants. He brings them in and gets them started. The manufacturing guys work on it and after five or six months they've made progress. Then the manufacturing guys come back and say, "You know boss, we know how to do this now. It's great. These guys really taught us a lot but we don't need the expense of these consultants any more. So if you want we can dump them in next year's budget."

As soon as they dump them, they start running backwards because it takes three to five years to get a guy who never had exposure to this to a level of competency that would allow him to push the ball forward if you pull away the consultants.

A three- to five-year period is like a college education.

BYRNE: It's just really a matter of exposure — of getting people to do kaizens.

Back when I was with Danaher, Shingijutsu worked exclusively for us for about four years. We were trying to think of how to spread this throughout Danaher. We understood it was a knowledge thing and that you had to hammer it from above, you couldn't let people choose this thing. You couldn't say, "Okay of the 13 companies, how many of you want to do it?" Because 12 of them would say no. Every six weeks we took the 13 presidents and all the VPs of operations to Japan for a week and we toured around factories and said, "Here is where we want to go. We want you to understand what other people are doing and how they do it."

When we got back we started an organization called the Presidents' Kaizens. Every six weeks we would take them to a different factory and do a three-day kaizen. We would come in on a Tuesday night and work Wednesday, Thursday and Friday. On Tuesday night we'd get everyone in early and give them a couple of hours of training on a subject and then break them into teams and go to the factory.

These factories had never been touched with a kaizen and it was interesting when we first showed up. The hourly workforce would say, "Wait a minute. What do you guys think you're going to do here? We've been working here for 15 years and 20 years and you don't know our business you've never been here before. You're only going to be here for three days. Come on, give us a break. You can't do anything in three days." By the end of three days, the same hourly workers would say, "You're not really going home today are you?" And we'd say, "Three days ago you told us to get lost and we couldn't help you. Why are you asking?" "Because you accomplished more in the last three days than we've accomplished in the last five years and couldn't you stick around for another week?" Then they'd say, "Hey, you're not going to go home and leave us with them, are you?"

These people understood the problems; they understood what was wrong. They had told their managers for years and the managers would say, "Yeah, yeah, yeah, yeah, I can't do that right now and I don't believe you. Don't tell me. I know better. We're not going that way."

We created a very good network of the presidents talking to each other and they all learned just how much you could accomplish in a short period of time. When they went back home and their people told them, "No, we can't do that," they could say, "Hey, listen, I was just on four different kaizens and this is what we accomplished so don't even try and tell

You can't let people choose this.

How do you get people thinking in a different way?

I personally did all the kaizen training.

me that you can't do this."

The whole thing is just a long training program to get people thinking in a different way.

Do you still spend time on the factory floor?

BYRNE: I started with a lot of time on the factory floor here, but as we've grown, we've bought about 22 different companies and with every new company we buy, I'm on the factory floor and do the first week of kaizen. If it's a sizeable company, I'll commit to three or four months or five months of going back one week a month doing kaizens.

Is it easy to transform a company that you've purchased?

BYRNE: It's always the same. It's a people issue. We can transform them all. But if you happen to get really good guys who understand it fairly soon, you'll just go faster and it's easier. If you get guys who are still resistant and who are not that good, you'll still get there because we don't give anybody the choice. If you give people the choice, you're asking for a problem. Once you get somebody who has operated this way as opposed to batch, they would never go back. They would never be happy going back into a batch environment because they couldn't deal with it any more.

We bought a company on the West Coast two years ago from a Fortune 500 New York Stock Exchange listed company of $3 billion in size. It was a product line acquisition for us for one of our subsidiary companies. It was a $12 million company with 88 people and it had lost money for five years in a row for this big company. The first day myself and the president of the subsidiary went in and got all of the employees in the cafeteria and said, "Hi, we're Wiremold. We just bought you and here's what Wiremold is about and our philosophy and how we run the company." We handed out some Wiremold shirts to everybody, took a coffee break and then gave them three hours of kaizen training.

I personally did all the kaizen training. I took them through the terms, the philosophy and how we're going to go from batch to one-piece flow. After lunch, we put together two kaizen teams. I was leading one and the president of the subsidiary was leading another. This particular factory had four or five of these 60 to 80 feet-long conveyor belt assembly lines with people sitting on either side of them with the product in between them. By 4:00 that afternoon, I had them totally dismantle one of these 80-foot long conveyor assembly lines grab a forklift, drag it into the parking lot and throw it away.

By noon the next day, we had moved the whole thing into a small cell that took up less than half to the space and we'd gone from 10 people down to six. We couldn't make the same output the next day, but within two weeks we were back to the same output with six people versus 10.

The second night we went out to dinner with the plant manager who we kept and he said, "You know, that was kind of dramatic. Does this mean I don't have to write the 18-page monthly plant report any more?" And we looked at each other, and I said, "Bob, are you going to read that if he writes it?" And Bob said, "No, I probably wouldn't read it. Would you read it?" And I said, "Hell, I'd never read something like that, why would I read something like that? We'd rather have you spend your time on the floor kaizening this mess you created in the first place."

Within one hour, we cut the floor space in half.

Within one year he cut the floor space in half, the inventory in half, cut the people down by 30 percent and we went from that company losing money for five years to making 14 percent operating margin the next year. If you know that you're going to do this and you know how to go about it and you start it on day one, you can quickly transform just about any company. People will jump into this culture very rapidly. We'll lose a few along the way that just refuse, but at the end of the day if they couldn't see this, then you wanted to lose them anyway, you're never going to convert them, so it was never a loss.

Is it inevitable that lean will become the operational mode of production in the United States?

BYRNE: Over time that is true. If you want to compete with me and you are doing batch and I'm doing lean, then over time, I'm going to kill you. I'm going to take your market share. You just don't have a chance.

You won't be able to compete with me.

But for some period of time you can have two-and-a-half or three inventory turns. If there is enough margin in the industry and there is growth for both of us, you can be a pain-in-the-neck competitor to me for quite some time. But as I go through cycles, you won't be able to compete with me because what will happen is that in order to have a short lead time, you'll have to keep adding inventory, which is more investment. You're going to need more space and more people. I don't need any of that stuff. My costs are much lower than yours. I'll be able to tell the customer that I can give them a two-day turnaround and the other guy is promising six weeks.

We're now trying to teach our distributor partners how to turn their inventory of our product over 10 times because most of them are running an MRP system. Most distributors are very traditional and tend to turn it only three times. A good guy might turn it five or six times. We're saying, "Hey, wait a minute. We can show you how to turn this stuff 10 to 15 times. Wouldn't you like to do that?"

An electrical distributor doesn't make a lot of margin. The whole industry makes 2 percent pretax. That is nothing. So how they manage their asset base, which is almost all inventory in a few warehouses, is really critical to them.

Yet most of the manufacturers in our industry are trying to load them up with product. They're saying, "If you buy a trailer load, I'll give you another five off." They're trying to sell them trailer loads because their manufacturing process makes 50 trailer loads at a crack.

But they don't need a trailer load. They don't even need a tenth of a

Why carry four months of inventory when I can show you how to carry two weeks' worth?

We had to teach our customers how to order in a different way.

trailer load. What they need is a small amount of stuff and spin it a lot. Why would you carry four months' worth if I can show you how to carry two weeks' worth?

How hard is it to sell the idea to your customers?
BYRNE: It's always been a hard sell. If I go back to my Jake Brake days when George Koenigsaecker was working for me running Jake Brake, we were an awful supplier to engine companies like Cummins and Caterpillar. As we got better, the next logical step was to talk to the customer because we could make every product every day, but he was ordering in big batches once a month. Why did he do that? Because we taught him to do it that way because our performance was so lousy. Now that our performance was better, we had to teach him to order in a different way.

We started with Caterpillar, and they were ordering big batches once a month. And we said, "How about if you order once a week?"

We would go and tell them why it was logical and they would understand it and say we'll try it. In about a month or two they would be back saying, "This doesn't work for our MRP and all of our computer systems. We're going to have to go back to once per month." They went back for a period but we kept selling them and they tried it again. You had to work with them in order to show them how to order once a week.

When we got them down to once a week, we said, "Let's do this a couple of times per week and then three times a week." Then we tried to get them to order every day. They understood fundamentally that it was good for them, but their systems and processes weren't set up for this.

It's the same for an electrical distributor. When we tell them that we want them to turn our inventory 10 or 15 times, they understand instantly that that is a good thing, particularly the owners. They ask, "How am I going to do it?" You have to teach them down to the right levels in their organization. You might get the owner to say fine, but if you don't train the guy who is ordering stuff every day off MRP to treat us differently, the computer spits it out and he orders it once per month.

How able are electrical distribution customers at handling a lean replenishment system?
BYRNE: The distributor with a low margin looks at a measurement that is called gross margin return on investment. They're really using the gross margin that they make on your product and the inventory that they carry in order to calculate a ratio. It's a complicated calculation, but a ratio of 1.2 times is pretty good. It says the gross margin they make on your product is about 1.2 times the amount of inventory they have to carry, as a rough calculation. Anyone in the 1.2 range is considered a pretty good supplier. Below that, there is a problem because they have to carry too much inventory or their margins are low.

If you take their inventory turns from three times to 10, all of a sudden, gross margin return on investment jumps up to two-and-a-half. Now you're almost off the charts of anybody that they would buy from. On their measurement criteria you have become probably the best vendor that they have not by a little bit, but by quite a lot.

What we've found is that as we teach these guys how to bring inventory down, they can also spread it out by carrying more odd fittings and a bigger array of stuff. As a result, they get to be known in their town as the guy who, when you need the odd Wiremold fitting, you can always call and he has it.

We've had guys come back to us and say, "We started doing this and my gross margin on investment went way up but also my sales grew, my margins grew and everything got better because people started coming to me looking for these products. It's great for them and it's great for us."

Right now, they all order on MRP and so they order nothing, nothing, nothing, then order three months' worth. That's how MRP works. If a bunch of them happen to order their three months' worth on the same day, we get big spikes and that becomes a nightmare for us to make some of this stuff because we don't carry much inventory.

The more we can teach them to order every day, and turn their inventory 10 or 15 times or higher, the better for us, the smoother the incoming order patterns are for us and the easier it is for us to satisfy what they need on a daily basis.

Is there a good MRP system that deals with the lean approach?
BYRNE: Not that I know of.

Are companies better off junking their MRP systems?
BYRNE: Yes. We got off of it pretty early and then went to a card system and that was a nightmare for quite some time because it wasn't a real good one. It was spotty. We had lots of fits and starts over kanban, which was a big issue for us. That's working pretty well now.

Does kanban migrate from being something other than cards?
BYRNE: It will probably still be card based.

Is there a good kanban software program?
BYRNE: No. We started out going to Toyota's kanban [software] system. We were the only guy in the United States who was not a Toyota supplier or tied into Toyota that was using their system. But we couldn't get the software support out of Japan. So this past year we switched and created our own version of it that we can support and grow.

Can the Internet provide leverage in the lean system?
BYRNE: Most distributors bar code scan items as they go out the door. We would like for them to convert that into a memo to us and we'll consider that an order and we'll accumulate everything they're selling every week and ship it to them as replenishment. We used to ship our

The more we can teach them to order every day, the better for us.

products on common carriers, but we implemented our own trucks and we supply 60 or 70 percent of our distributors every week at a certain time. We're very consistent on that schedule. They can count on the fact that the Wiremold truck will be there between 10:00 and noon every Thursday.

One of our early first-starting-out business philosophies was make every product every day. I don't have an order for every product every day, so I'm not literally going to make it. I just have to be prepared so that if I get an order I can make every product every day.

Make every product every day.

Is the Internet a big deal in all of this? Is it an enabler?
BYRNE: Not so far. We'd like to be able to get orders over the Internet and that will speed up the information flow, but you still physically have to make the stuff. You physically have to move it. You physically have to buy parts. Things are still done physically.

We buy parts from suppliers based on kanban. The cardboard vendor comes in the morning and he delivers what we ordered yesterday in the afternoon and we give him a physical fistful of kanban cards. We had gone to his location and done kaizens to show him how to deal with these kanban cards and put them on the next bundle of product. In the afternoon, he'll come back and give us bundles of cardboard with the kanban cards on these bundles that we gave him in the morning.

So what do we need the Internet for? We want to physically give him these cards so he can physically put them on the product so we can keep track of them. In cases like that we don't really need it. But I can see some uses for the Internet with our communication with other suppliers, like our steel supplier, who is farther away and we have to communicate with him electronically.

At the end of the day, it's all physical.

What do we need the Internet for?

Is your inventory turn figure the key measure for your business?
BYRNE: We use about five or six measures and if you want to say that's too many, I would tell you to use only two measures: inventory turns and customer service. If you could have customer service going up and inventory turns going up at the same time, I can just about guarantee you that you are doing a good job every place else.

That is the antithesis of how most people think about business. Most people accept low inventory turns as a necessary evil in order to have good customer service. They think about it in the exact opposite way.

We found that the more we can turn inventory, the faster we can turn it, the better our customer service gets. In order to turn it that well and have good customer service, you have to have good quality, good costs and good productivity because those things are all linked.

In our language internally, we see inventory as the root of all evil, because it is. It's only there for bad reasons. If you were better you wouldn't need to have it. When you go to a huge Toyota factory — and huge is

We see inventory as the root of all evil, because it is.

like a city — and you ask them how much inventory they have and they hang their head and say, "We are very baaad today, we have point eight days of inventory and we're supposed to have point five." You just want to go out into the parking lot and shoot yourself. Then you go onto the floor and see it.

People around here are running around with three or four months' worth. Look at a company like Boeing. When they finish their product it flies away. Not too long ago, they were turning inventory one time — one time. If they turned it 10 times, they would free up $15 billion in cash. And you ask: What's wrong with management's thinking that they wouldn't be interested in turning it 10 times and generating $15 billion? Why aren't shareholders screaming for that?

The reason for it is they don't believe it, and even if they believed it, they don't know how to do it. They've got a whole organization that is telling them it can't be done. How's one CEO going to go against this whole organization that is telling them that this can't be done because they are Boeing and they are different?

Is there a good number for inventory turns?
BYRNE: It depends on what you're selling and whom you're selling it to. If you're selling to OEMs, your turns should be over 20 maybe 25. It could be even higher than that, and I calculate inventory turns on total FIFO inventory, which includes everything. Some people want to talk about inventory turns of only finished goods and they want to slice down into some layer. We could tell you huge numbers if you want to slice it like that, but we look at it as total FIFO inventory, period.

I would say if you're selling into distribution, 20 is a possible number. We sell to distributors and we find that is a much more difficult thing, because the order patterns can be very erratic and they want the stuff right away. We're at 15 now and our initial target is 20, but the distribution part makes it difficult.

We try to introduce lots of new products and with new products, you wind up putting some of that in stock and all of a sudden, if it takes three or four months for that product to get off the ground, your turns are going backwards. You have stuff sitting there that isn't doing anything.

Did your life change after your story was told by James Womack in the book *Lean Thinking*?
BYRNE: Not really. The kaizen world in the U.S. is a network. I know a lot of these guys because a lot of them used to work for me. We had a lot of requests for factory tours just off my personal network. The requests from people wanting to come through here jumped up after Womack's book, but we had a very simple solution to that. We said, "We know that unless the CEO leads this it won't be successful, so if you want to come here, you have to bring your CEO."

That cut out almost all the manufacturing tourists. We didn't even

Our initial target is 20 turns.

Unless the CEO leads this, it won't be successful.

have to worry about it. We said that's our rule and if you don't want to abide by it, you can't come, period. Most people couldn't do that.

The Parts Hotel
By Art Byrne

Welcome to the Parts Hotel
It's really quite the place!
We love our parts so very much
We give them lots of space

They come on in to get a rest
We treat them all the best
They lay about for weeks or months
Just waiting to go out

We love for them to gather dust
In this we really trust
And sometimes if we're lucky
They stay long enough to rust!

They have a lot of fun here
They make a lot of buddies
We feel we can sell them for more money
If they get a little cruddy

The hotel is really spacious
The racks go to the sky
If we understand the waste here
We'd all break down and cry

The parts fly in but don't go out
They hope that they'll grow old
I'm sure you'll understand this
Their only other option is to finally get sold
They really like the staff here
They treat them with such care
Especially Dame Barbie
And the hat that hides her hair

The location is also special
It's dark and out of the way
It's really pretty famous
They call it the ICA

But now the massive Parts Hotel
With its racks up to the ceiling
Has been exposed as massive waste
And has that shrinking feeling

Dame Barbie has responded well
The racks are coming down
Soon there will be no Parts Hotel
And no extra parts doing nothing by lying around

Byrne penned this poem shortly after Wiremold acquired Walker Systems Inc, and he toured that company's large inventory control area (ICA). Barbara Looney was manager of the ICA department.

DANAHER CORP. / LEAN HORIZONS

Danaher Corp., a diversified industrial conglomerate based in Washington, D.C., is one of the best-managed yet least-known U.S. industrial companies, ranking for some in stature with General Electric. The maker of Craftsman Tools for Sears has spent the past 13 years perfecting its Danaher Business System (DBS), which is founded upon the principles of the Toyota Production System.

Danaher is considered to be one of the most advanced companies in the United States in lean implementation. It has quietly gone about its business, shunning publicity and concentrating on serving its customers. The approximately 60 autonomous companies under Danaher's umbrella have one unifying characteristic: they have all deployed the Danaher Business System within their operations. This system "continuously strives to improve quality, delivery and cost," says Danaher. "The Danaher Business System can be found in every corner of Danaher operating units, not just on the shop floor. Customer service, finance and marketing all benefit from the application of DBS business tools."

Danaher's commitment to its lean production system continues to produce positive long-term returns, even in the difficult economy that engulfed manufacturers through 2001. The company's sales increased that year to $3.782 billion from $3.77 billion, and operating profits jumped to $572 million ($2.30 per share), up from $552 million ($2.23 per share) in 2000. The company generated $528 million in free cash flow in 2001, up from $424 million in 2000.

Danaher adopted the Toyota Production System in 1987 at its Jacobs Vehicle Systems division. The effort was led successfully by Mark DeLuzio, a financial executive, who then shifted to a senior position at Danaher and was the architect of the Danaher Business System. "I saw it from an administrative side and a shop floor side as well and was involved in all the early kaizens and went to Japan five zillion times," says DeLuzio. "I learned it from the bottom up."

DeLuzio not only developed a system that deployed lean tools, but he created an overarching strategy built upon "breakthrough objectives" and a "policy deployment" plan that kept managers focused on achieving results. DeLuzio recently retired from Danaher and has a new firm called Lean Horizons.

Don't focus on the lean tools.

Danaher is frequently mentioned as being one of the best examples of how an old industrial company can transform itself and become a high growth, high performance company by using lean techniques. How did you deploy lean throughout Danaher?

DeLUZIO: [Danaher CEO] George Sherman said, "Hey, you've been doing well with this at Jacobs, let's take it companywide." As we started looking at the corporation there were a couple of things missing. Jacobs' approach using the Toyota Production System was from a tool perspective. We were using Five-S and standard work and almost to our detriment we created a situation where the tools themselves became the objective. That was wrong and that is where a lot of companies today fail because they look at the tools themselves.

In order for lean to work, you have to have a business strategy. If you have a business strategy and understand your objectives then the lean tools will help achieve those objectives. But if you make lean the objective, you're going to fail. The idea that we had to drive policy deployment gave birth to the Danaher Business System. We simplified policy deployment and made it effective throughout the corporation. It's been almost a decade and Danaher is still using it. It's time tested and is still going strong.

In studying various implementations, have you found that even the Japanese have this problem of being too focused on tools and on lean being the objective?

DeLUZIO: There are people out there who are big in the lean world in the U.S. and still don't understand the strategy part. They feel that no matter what the situation, add a little lean and you're going to fix it. If you don't have a good business strategy, lean alone won't solve your problems.

What constitutes a sound business strategy in the adoption of lean?

DeLUZIO: You can apply lean to a buggy whip company and you're going to fail. If you have the wrong product and the wrong strategy, it doesn't matter. You have to look at the markets you're in, the business, your technology and your competitive advantage. I've seen some businesses without good strategies that have done very well with lean and did not perform. It's as simple as that.

Does lean help a company focus on strategy?

DeLUZIO: If they do it right, it forces them to understand how much value they are truly adding to their customer base; but without the fundamentals of strategic planning and the right business, it's useless.

You can apply lean to a buggy whip company and you're going to fail.

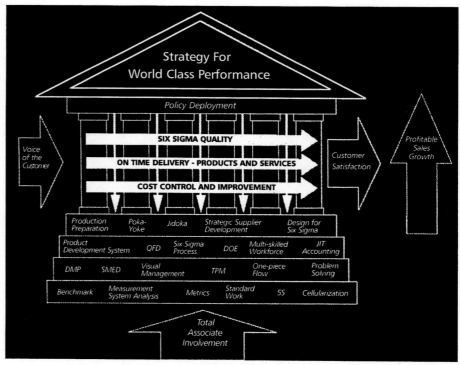

The Danaher Business System

Can you give me an example?

DeLUZIO: I had a president of a company call me a few years ago and he asked that we get involved with his company and within the first 10 minutes I could tell him that it didn't matter if he did lean in his company because he had a bad strategy. He had no leverage because of his size; he wasn't in the big catalogs like Granger; and he had no competitive advantage to speak of, zero. He truly believed that if he applied lean to the business, he'd kick butt. I said you might get some good leverage out of that, but you don't have a good business strategy and without that strategy, it's not going to work.

What advice do you have for companies that don't have a strategy?

DeLUZIO: The companies that really make it — like Danaher — have a good eclectic view of their company. They don't want to become just a manufacturing company. They aren't just marketing driven or engineering driven. They have a balance between all of those disciplines and come up with a good business solution. So it isn't just manufacturing and lean.

Quite frankly, there are a lot of manufacturing guys out there who don't understand strategy and conversely there are a lot of marketing guys out there who don't understand lean. You need a good mix. Danaher does a nice job of mixing the commercial side and the tactical side with lean and the Danaher Business System. It has a policy deployment process in place that really takes that strategy and drives it throughout the organization with breakthrough objectives and measurable quality, delivery, cost and growth objectives using the tools of lean to help achieve those business objectives. The objectives were what we were shooting for.

Veeder-Root, one of Danaher's divisions, went from selling hardware that monitors gasoline tanks to being a company that serviced the tanks. Is that an example of the strategic policy that you were in charge of putting in place at Danaher?

DeLUZIO: They could have sold their tank-level sensors and monitoring equipment to gas stations. But strategically, they said, the oil companies are very capital constrained and they cannot afford these systems. Veeder-Root was coming to them with a very expensive up-front hardware solution that was going to cost them a lot of money.

We determined that if we sold a service instead with an annuity payment scheduled over five to 10 years, it made it a lot more palatable. The equipment itself became part of that annuity payment so that there were no big cash outlays. It was very easy to get in with the oil companies. That is what I mean by strategy. Without that strategy, the company would not have weathered that storm.

Do you believe that only 1 percent of all manufacturers have adopted a lean strategy to grow their businesses?

Dahaner's policy deployment process takes that strategy and drives it throughout the organization.

Selling services is as important as selling equipment.

Be prepared to deal with big problems.

DeLUZIO: I agree on the numbers because lean exposes problems and is a pain in the butt to do. You have to be prepared to deal with big problems. Not a lot of companies even think in the right frame of mind to be able to go and deal with the problems in a fact-based manner. Many people like to hide behind problems and hide behind inventory.

How does a company overcome the hurdle of knowing their problems exist, but actually saying we have to address them?

DeLUZIO: It has to be a culture of how you think and how you deal with problems. One of the values at Danaher was that it was fact-based. We always made it tough on ourselves, even in the way we calculated parts-per-million rejects. We made the measure ugly. That was a cultural thing.

We made sure people were not hiding behind a problem and that they were dealing with the root cause. Even getting executives to understand what the root cause is takes a long time and requires a cultural shift.

How long does that shift take for a company that isn't running that way?

DeLUZIO: If a company is really maniacal about lean it takes two- to three-years to go from kindergarten to first grade. That's how tough it is.

Where is Danaher in the process?

DeLUZIO: I think they're still in grade school, but they are a lot better than most companies in the United States. I don't mean that in a negative way because they've done a lot of great things. It's just the hurdles are so high. I have seen companies in Japan that are turning inventory 300 times and Danaher's best company turns inventory 25 times.

How does Danaher go from 25 turns to 300?

DeLUZIO: The company at Danaher that is at 25 turns went from two to 25 and they've been at it for over a decade. That is why I'm saying how tough this is. The company we saw in Japan has been doing it for 35 years.

The mindset you have to have is a healthy dissatisfaction with the status quo.

People ask what kaizen and lean are all about and I say that the mindset you have to have is a healthy dissatisfaction with the status quo. You can't always be negative and beat yourself up, but you always have to understand that no matter what you've done, there is a better way. The fact that Toyota makes it ugly and they think they're not very good at lean is cultural because they realize that if they become complacent they're not going to get there.

What do you think GM faces, given that Toyota attitude?

DeLUZIO: I don't think they understand it. It scares me. It's my sincerest hope that the auto companies don't look at this like it's another FreeMarkets or another cost-cutting activity because they will miss the point. You do get cost savings with lean and that is a byproduct, but there are so many other things that happen that I hope they don't use this to beat the heck out of their suppliers. That will just give lean such a bad flavor.

What did it take to change the culture at Danaher?
DeLUZIO: Number one, this can't be a middle-management type of thing moving up. The top guys have to be totally committed to it. They have to become educated and when I say educated I mean benchmarking like you wouldn't believe: going to Japan, seeing the best companies, talking to people who are doing it and really spending time benchmarking and understanding.

They also have to become educated not only from a book sense but a hands-on sense in terms of participating because the light bulbs don't turn on until you actually do it. It's not until their light bulbs go on and they truly internalize it that they will start creating a culture.

At the end of the day people do what the boss is expecting them to do.

At the end of the day people do what the boss is expecting them to do. If the boss only drives cost then there will be no results. They have to be measured on quality, delivery and how they solve problems. Policy deployment is all about creating sustainable business processes that yield results.

A lot of managers today are only being measured on results and they are not being measured on creating the business process. People say, "You just delivered a new product in 16 months, that was fantastic." Nobody says to them: "Show me the business process that yielded that result and I want to make sure it's sustainable so we can repeat it again next time."

The whole measurement system and how we measure people on results is our biggest problem. The senior guys have to understand that. They have to be asking for the sustainable business process that gets the result as well as the result itself. That is the culture shift that has to happen. Without that happening at the very top level, it's not going to take over.

And Danaher had that support?
DeLUZIO: We had that with George Sherman and the Rales brothers. They saw it work and they weren't manufacturing guys and for non manufacturing guys this stuff makes a lot more sense than to manufacturing people and the reason is there are so many new paradigms involved.

Things are going to get worse before they get better.

When I start my training sessions, I ask everybody to write their name with their dominant hand and then I have them switch hands and have them write their name again. I say, "Do you see how uncomfortable and how odd that was? That is how lean is going to feel to you initially. It's going to feel that odd because it really is counter intuitive."

One of the things I say is that things are going to get worse before they get better because lean doesn't create problems it exposes them. People who don't understand say that lean causes all of these problems because we've never had these problems before. The reality is you really did.

Did it get worse at Danaher before it got better?
DeLUZIO: It got worse at every company at Danaher. There was a lot of chaos in every company.

How did Danaher and all of its divisions overcome that chaos?
DeLUZIO: It was management persistence and fallout on the leadership side. People aren't going to get it and you have to make that change at the top. That is just a fact of life.

My approach with a lot of the new companies we acquired was I'd sit down with the CEO and ask him what he was really concerned about. Are you concerned that I'm going to screw up your 3 percent operating income? Or are you concerned that I'm going to bring your two inventory turns down to one and a half? Or am I going to mess up your 80,000 parts-per-million quality reject rate? I'd say guys, come on, if you keep doing the same things over and over again expecting different results, you're crazy.

What would you generally hear when you asked those questions?
DeLUZIO: It was usually silence.

Do you have to have tough love in order for them to change?
DeLUZIO: There is a mix. You have to do things tactfully. I really don't believe the in-your-face things works.

Was it to your advantage to know how the process plays so that you could provide guidance as companies went through the difficult period of transition?
DeLUZIO: When we did this at Jake Brake, we had nobody to go to because nobody in the United States was doing it. The only people we could point to were companies in Japan. As a result, there were all the excuses such as it was cultural.

As we began to gain momentum at Danaher, we were able to point to the companies at Danaher that had successes. But even then people were making excuses. They say, "They're in a different industry, our company is different." And I'd say, "You are truly different: they're making money and you're losing money. So when are you going to get on board?"

It wasn't that bad because we created a culture in which new acquisitions knew they were going to do the Danaher Business System and it was just a question of how.

Did you find that the implementation changed with each company?
DeLUZIO: You can't take a cookie-cutter approach. Value-stream mapping and policy deployment work hand in hand because there is not

If you keep doing the same things over and over again expecting different results, you're crazy.

You have to do things tactfully. In-your-face doesn't work.

an approach that says do A, then do B, then do C. There are some things I wouldn't recommend doing first, second and third on a macro basis. But when you get into it, you start asking, "Do I do a SMED [single minute exchange of dies]? Do I do standard work? Do I cellularize?"

The policy deployment and value-stream map help you identify where and when you should be doing those things. One of the things we learned over the years is that every company is different and every company will have a different implementation strategy.

Is the value-stream map one of the key tools to deploy immediately?
DeLUZIO: What we do first is look at the strategy and try to figure out two, three or four breakthrough objectives for a company. Then we deploy policy deployment.

What are some of the breakthrough objectives?
DeLUZIO: They change from company to company, but an example of one could be as simple as drastically improving on-time delivery. To get a company that is delivering at 20 percent on time to 85 to 90 percent in one year is nowhere near world class but it is a breakthrough.

Another could be a huge quality objective — taking defects from 125,000 parts per million to six sigma. Then there are growth objectives. Quality, delivery, cost and growth are the four main categories of breakthroughs.

Do you produce a written goals document?
DeLUZIO: The policy deployment process is a very rigid process and it is what made the Danaher Business System a system. It documents what you want to do on a three- to five-year basis while reducing it to an annual basis for the assignment of responsibilities and targets.

Those annual objectives are then deployed down into the organization. You could be deploying to a functional team, a multifunctional team, a function itself, a person or any number of those. Then there is a linkage from all the way down to the lower end of the organization all the way back up so that people who are working three or four levels down are working on the things that are necessary to achieve the strategy.

The other element of policy deployment is deciding what you're not going to do. A lot of well-known lean practitioners today are pursuing 25 objectives. There is no way a company can be successful with 25 objectives. It's just too much, and when everything is important, nothing is important. There has to be an A, B and C ranking of those. You can't attack every problem facing your company, like absenteeism, safety, delivery, quality and square footage.

But each of those is important in its own right.
DeLUZIO: You can't argue with any of them. But how can you do them all? How do you prioritize your day?

Every company will have a different implementation strategy.

Quality, delivery, cost and growth are the four main categories of breakthroughs.

Don't you think people need help to do this?

DeLUZIO: I love the guys at Shingijutsu, they are great, but one of the things I've always said is that — as much as I love them and they trained me — they are not business people. These guys were middle-level managers and engineers who became very good at the Toyota Production System and are now sitting down with the CEO of a $4-billion company telling him how to run his business. That does not compute. That is where the strategy piece and policy deployment are never talked about with Shingijutsu because they don't understand that. We would use them for very good tool training but don't ask them to do strategy.

How hard is it to bring it down to the guy on the shop floor?

DeLUZIO: That is the beauty of the policy deployment process. It gives you the tactical hands-on methodology to drive it right down to the janitor and he'll know every day when he wakes up and goes to work how he is going to get measured and what is important to the business. If you do it right, he'll be able to say that what he is doing in his job every day is going to help that objective. If he is able to say that on the shop-floor level, then you know you've got it.

The janitor knows every day when he wakes up what is important to the business.

The other aspect of lean that proves to be so difficult is the back end of a company's operation: human resources, accounting, financing, engineering, product development, marketing and ordering. How hard is it to deploy lean throughout that part of a company?

DeLUZIO: It's extremely difficult to implement. Every function within a company is going to change. If it doesn't change, you haven't done lean. For example, the traditional accounting systems that we have set up are geared toward SEC and IRS statutory requirements. We take the output from these systems and we say manage your business with them. Yet they are motivating the wrong behaviors because they're asking you to do the wrong things.

Absorption accounting, for example, and purchase price variance drive the wrong behaviors. They're anti lean. When you tell this to the finance guy, he says they are good measures. No they're not. Again, it's like writing with your left hand. You have to get the accounting guys to change.

You have to get the HR people to change.

You have to get the HR people to change. HR people need to understand that the work environment will be truly different in that we're asking people to do a lot of different jobs and they're going to be multiskilled. We have to put reward systems in place so there is an incentive for them to learn new jobs. If we don't do that we're going to have a lot of problems.

How the sales and marketing guys take orders definitely impacts the shop. If they take batch orders and allow their customers to order once per month to buy three months of supply, then you'll never be able to level the load in manufacturing. Level loading is almost impossible without your sales department changing how they incentivize the sales force, and how they manage their distributors and their customers. Every single function has to get on the same page.

How do you get these people on board?
DeLUZIO: They have to be on the shop floor when you do the first kaizen. The only way they understand is if they get out there and do it. I had a sales guy one time tell me, "Mark I never knew what I was doing to the shop floor until I got on this kaizen."

Do all these functions revolve around manufacturing?
DeLUZIO: They should, but not always. It is amazing to look at how much time the accounting function spends on things you don't need. The first thing you have to ask these guys is who is your customer? The accounting function will have several, the IRS, the SEC, corporate and several other different customers but rarely do they say they have an internal customer.

I like to use the lean tools in the administrative environments to reduce the amount of time it takes to do the statutory stuff so that the administrative people can spend more time being knowledge workers and add value to the business and the functions. Instead of taking two weeks to close your books, here's your breakthrough, close in three days. And let's kaizen the accounts payable process so that instead of three people doing the job you have one person. Then take those two people and upgrade them and have them work on design teams doing target costing and proactive things that will help the business rather than just being scorekeepers. That is the kind of mentality you need in order to change.

Does this work successfully at Danaher?
DeLUZIO: Not always. But this is a real mature look at the business and not everybody gets there. When I say Danaher is still in grade school that's what I'm talking about.

How do you convince someone in the finance department to change the way they do their books?
DeLUZIO: I went up to a company in Massachusetts and the president said to me, "Mark, we're trying to get rid of labor reporting. We know it's the wrong thing, but we can't convince the finance guy. You've got a finance background, can you help him?"

We figured out that the accounting guy was just worried about his variance accounts. He was the only one who looked at them. I looked at the president and said, "Do you use this?" And he said no, and I turned to the accounting guy and said, "Well there is your customer and he doesn't use it, so get rid of it." They stopped their labor reporting in their machine shop and saved $100,000 a year in time and effort recording those transactions.

> *It is amazing to look at how much time the accounting function spends on things you don't need.*

Is that a lean process?

DeLUZIO: Absolutely, because the activity was non-value added. It was wasteful. Their operators were sitting at their computers for half an hour a day. My definition of lean is the maniacal pursuit of the elimination of waste from every business process. That's it.

Lean is not only about the physical surroundings of how you handle materials, the shop floor and the machines. When you do a kaizen, you are kaizening your mind because you are changing the way you think. Everything is going to be a byproduct of how you think. The key is how leaders think about their business. That is what you are changing. That is really the kaizen.

How long did it take for you to get the financial systems aligned with lean operating practices?

DeLUZIO: About two years. The thing about finance is you cannot lead it, you have to follow the changes in the company. You can't go make changes in your financial systems without the company making the changes first.

A lot of companies are doing their strategic planning and are deciding to outsource their manufacturing. Is that a good way to get rid of their batch-and-queue problems rather than having to go through the turmoil associated with a lean implementation?

DeLUZIO: You don't get rid of anything. You're handing over designs that were probably not leaned out anyway and they still have inherent problems within them. You're adding a margin somewhere to the costs.

I'm not saying outsourcing is the wrong thing because there are things you should outsource if they're not your core competency. But for the companies that outsource manufacturing and then beat up the supplier all they are doing is moving the problem.

Yet with much shorter product cycle times, most companies in the electronics sector are outsourcing all of their manufacturing.

DeLUZIO: Many companies think of manufacturing in terms of buying large increments of capacity. But if you think of lean in a machine design sense, you are purchasing small increments of capacity that is flexible and can be quickly changed over. It can be easily adaptable to new designs, and can be easily movable within your plant so that you can add an extra 10 percent of capacity without any problem. Your investment is small — you're not adding another $500,000 machine to add just 10 percent more capacity.

A lot of the companies that are making these outsourcing decisions haven't thought that through from a machine design point of view. You can really build a superior competitive advantage through machine design.

When you do a kaizen, you are kaizening your mind.

Companies that out-source manufacturing and then beat up the supplier all they are doing is moving the problem.

Any company can go out and buy the same materials and equipment and compete for the same labor. But if I can build a competitive advantage with my equipment, then all of a sudden I have something you don't have and I can take you to the cleaners.

We had a case in Danaher where we bought a huge $1-million piece of equipment and we found out that the guy we bought it from sold one exactly like it to one of our competitors, even after we gave him a lot of the ideas for upgrades. Because we did not build our own internal capability we didn't have a competitive advantage. Building your internal capability using 3-P — the production preparation process — is the key.

Is it inevitable that manufacturing companies will move towards a lean system?

DeLUZIO: I think it is. It's common sense. I actually think common sense is misnamed, it's not common.

Is Six Sigma covering the same territory?

DeLUZIO: Some of the tools of Six Sigma can be very powerful, but companies like GE and AlliedSignal have elected to create cultures around a tool. If you really look at Six Sigma, it's not a culture, it's a tool. It's not a philosophy, it's a tool. It's a problem-solving process with some very sophisticated tools and techniques. Six Sigma is no different from any of the lean tools.

The more important questions to ask are: What is your business process? What is your problem? What is your strategic objective? What are the tools you're going to need to achieve your objective?

If I'm digging a hole and am using a shovel, if I hit a rock, I use a pick and if I need a stick of dynamite, I'll use it. But I'm going to use the tool that will help me achieve the objective. Maybe it's a Pareto analysis, maybe it's a 5-Why, maybe it's a design of experiment, maybe it's standard work, maybe its SMED.

Six Sigma and lean can work together, but companies that look at them as an either/or make a mistake.

What about a company that deploys just-in-time delivery as a way of doing business? Isn't that company deploying a lean philosophy?

DeLUZIO: JIT is used synonymously with lean. When you look at the definition of JIT, it's the right product at the right time at the right place and that is what lean is trying to do.

So are all of the companies that have gone to a JIT system basically lean?

DeLUZIO: Unfortunately, a lot of the JIT world focuses on the supplier side and it's basically an approach to move inventory back to the supply base. As a result, nothing gets leaned out. Nothing gets improved. All the waste is moved back to another level.

Common sense is misnamed. It's not common.

Six Sigma and lean can work together.

When you were implementing lean at Danaher, how hard was it to get buy-in from the shop-floor workers?

DeLUZIO: I have had less problems with operating folks than I've had with managers. The operating folks are pretty smart and logical especially when they see something that is going to make their life easier. I have had operators come up to me and say if you go back to the way we used to do it, I'm quitting. Their life is chaos until you can straighten it out. They don't like to live in chaos every day.

What types of behaviors must leaders exhibit in order for lean business practices to stick?

DeLUZIO: One of the problems is they try to delegate it and that doesn't work. If you really want to drive change you can't just say go out and be a better leader. You have to actually describe the behaviors that leaders need to exhibit in order to support the effort.

What are some of those behaviors?

DeLUZIO: You must participate in hands-on kaizens. You must do at least six to 12 hands-on kaizens in the first year. Presidents and vice presidents have to learn how to walk the talk. First it shows support, but second, their light bulbs are going to get turned on if it's done right.

Then they must participate in kaizen report-outs. All the kaizen teams have report-outs on Friday afternoons. They have to participate in those. They can't ignore those.

Another one is that as you go through your facilities, make sure you spend time on the shop floor. Go through the design engineering office. Ask questions. Look for metrics. Look for visuals. It's your opportunity to find out what's going on and to show support.

I had a president who actually went into one of his divisions and his total trip to this company was the conference room. He didn't go to the shop floor. So I pulled him aside and said you have to spend time on the shop floor. You have to be able to walk out there and spend time there because you are sending a message by not going out there. What you don't do is just as important as what you do do. Facility-wide reviews are important.

The leaders must learn the tools well enough to teach them. You must learn them that well because then nobody is able to snow you and you're showing how important it is to you.

Become maniacal about learning about lean. I say you have to read six books annually on lean business practices, at least six. One every other month is not a big deal.

Benchmarking other companies is another behavior. Take those benchmarking trips to Japan. Go to Toyota in Georgetown, Kentucky. Visit Freudenberg-NOK or Wiremold or whoever will let you in their doors. It is absolutely key that you personally proactively go out and benchmark. You have to do it.

Leaders must participate in hands-on kaizens.

Leaders must learn the tools well enough to teach them.

You have to talk about lean blackbelts, or whatever you want to call them.

Another way for them to behave is pure thought process in terms of insisting on facts and data and not on opinions.

They need to really drive process improvements and not just results.

Another is to provide the support and resources necessary to build your own internal lean capability within your business. You have to talk about lean blackbelts, or whatever you want to call them — lean champions.

You have to build that capability internally so that you're developing two, three, four or five people who are learning these tools. They have to go to school and bring that knowledge internally and drive it. If you don't provide that kind of support system it won't work.

FREUDENBERG-NOK

Freudenberg-NOK, created in 1989 as the U.S. combination of Freudenberg & Co. of Germany and the NOK Group of Japan, has a chairman who is adamant about lean production and management systems. CEO Joseph Day is convinced that lean is the only viable solution available to the automotive industry that is bedeviled by deep structural problems. Day's fervent belief led him to create a new company in 2001 called the Lean Center that will sell Freudenberg's lean knowledge to companies.

Since its adoption of lean practices in 1992, Freudenberg-NOK has quadrupled its U.S. sales to over $1 billion, growing at an average annual rate of 15 percent. It has conducted more than 8,000 kaizens in the Americas; reduced its defect rate from more than 2,000 parts per million to less than 50 with some plants at less than 10 and others at less than three. It has reduced work-in-process inventory by 80 percent; increased labor productivity by 25 percent per year; and has expanded its revenue per 1,000 square feet of factory space by 350 percent. The company projects revenues of $1.5 billion by 2005.

For every manufacturer that has adopted the lean culture, "there are literally thousands that still don't get it," says Day, whose company manufactures sealing, anti-vibration and elastomeric products for the auto industry. "The sub-tier suppliers need to understand that the practice of lean systems is so critically important that I believe automakers will soon make it a requirement of their vendors. It's not that far away!"

Included in this interview with Day are comments from Tom Faust, who is in charge of Freudenberg-NOK's Get Rid Of Waste Through Team Harmony (GROWTTH) program and who is also president of the Lean Center.

The Big 3 automakers currently spend about $6 billion on warranty a year or $500 per new car sold.

Is the automobile industry in trouble if it doesn't adopt lean production techniques?

DAY: If we fall back to selling 14 million units, we have a crisis on our hands. The business model does not allow the industry and its supply community to make money at the peak of its volume. Now that just doesn't make any sense. But those are the facts of life.

The Big 3 automakers currently spend about $6 billion — that's billion with a "B" — on warranty a year. You do the math. In round figures, $6 billion in warranty divided by 12 million vehicles sold by the Big 3 — that's an average cost savings of $500 per new car sold. Perhaps the industry should move its focus away from confrontational negotiations for tenth of a penny price reduction per component and move into partnership solutions that attack this $6-billion problem.

The Japanese vehicle industry on the other hand has significant advantage as their warranty costs per new car sold are perhaps less than $75 per car. A big difference between the U.S. and Japan is sharing technology and the Japanese partnerships that meet target prices, normally 8 percent to 15 percent down at the launch of a new vehicle instead of during the vehicle life. In the Japanese case, the costs really come out up front and therefore the price pressure during the vehicle life is very different.

However, the biggest, biggest difference is not generally understood in the U.S. market. The Japanese vehicle manufacturers demand that their suppliers practice lean business principles. It's not an option. Either you learn and practice lean or you're kicked out of the supply base.

Why can't the U.S. industry make money at the height of the market?

DAY: The vehicle manufacturing executives have the sense — and I

The big auto companies continue to ignore $45 billion in waste in this $400-billion industry.

believe they are dead wrong on this — that the added value component of the automotive industry is fixed. Given that idea, they have the sense that they are not going to be able to make incremental profit unless they can drag it out of the income statements and off the balance sheets of their supply community.

For reasons I don't understand, they continue to ignore what I describe as being a $45 billion in waste in this $400-billion industry. The reason I say it's $45 billion is because I'm pretty good at this stuff and I still have in my own company more than 8 percent of my sales as waste and it could be as much as 10 percent. That $45 billion in waste represents three times the average income that the industry has generated, not just the vehicle manufacturers, but the entire supply chain.

Using lean production and management techniques, the automobile industry could have produced the 2002 car models with 20 percent less manufacturing cost, 40 percent less capital investment, 50 percent greater labor productivity, 60 percent higher quality and in 30 percent less time.

Why aren't the big OEMs doing something about it?

DAY: Because they're spending too much time trying to bully the margin out of their supply base and they're not spending enough time reducing waste in their own systems. Secondly, the supply community has consistently rolled over and conceded to the price requests that the industry keeps putting on them and in the absence of the supply community saying, "Hey! Enough is enough," they're going to keep asking for price breaks. It's like, "Why not ask, they might give it to you."

Lean systems are rare in the second tier supplier ranks and virtually nonexistent in the lower tiers. The result: Japanese auto companies continue to grow their market share at the U.S. companies' expense.

Companies that don't adopt lean manufacturing practices won't make the automakers' purchasing cut.

Companies that don't adopt lean manufacturing practices won't make the automakers' purchasing cut. It won't take very long for that requirement to cascade down the tiers of the supply chain because each company's leanness ultimately depends on the leanness of its own suppliers.

Does Freudenberg stand up to this bullying?

DAY: Oh absolutely. We are able to beat them off the majority of the time. We are able to negotiate value and then the customer is ultimately willing to pay for that value. They're not happy about that, but more often than not they are willing to accept the value proposition that we bring to bear.

Quality dictates success.

DAY: Our quality levels are at the very top. The robustness and reproducibility and consistency of our products is superb. That is a point of difference relative to our competition. It all adds up to less warranty risk to our customers.

Why don't you think lean manufacturing has taken off in the automotive supply chain?

DAY: The execution of lean costs money. You have to pay somebody to teach you how to do it. But the industry is not recognizing that the payback on the discretionary spending you need to install lean is probably less than four months. We are returning on average three times the cost than we're spending to install lean. Freudenberg-NOK is spending $7 million in discretionary money to continue to push lean and Six Sigma through our organization. This calendar year before give-backs to our customers, we'll save $31 million. Why doesn't the rest of the industry take the step and spend the money and save the money? There are not enough people out there to teach them how to do it.

There are not enough people out there to teach them how to do it.

What do you think of some of the lean training organizations, like Shingijutsu?

DAY: It's six guys and they're running around the world helping Porsche and Wiremold. They were the launch leader for us at Freudenberg-NOK. But in looking at their ability to impact the automotive business, you can't even find a ripple.

What major roadblocks need to be overcome for a company to get on the lean journey?

DAY: It needs senior management sponsorship. There has to be a willingness to focus attention on execution and there has to be a continuing and passionate commitment to it.

Toyota seems to be a company in overdrive, taking market share every year from all of its rivals due to its lean production system.

DAY: Toyota invented and discovered the concept and then mandated it to their vendors with the idea that if they didn't do it, they couldn't play in their game. But Toyota taught them how to do it over the past 35 years and these vendors have continued to get better and better and better at the practice. In the American market, we now have this enormous need to be trained, but the Big Three and most of the large tier-ones don't have the ability to teach their vendors how to do it. So there has to be a different mechanism for getting that done.

How far along is Freudenberg-NOK on the lean journey?

DAY: After eight years of practice I've learned that there are six stages in the lean journey. There aren't 10 and there aren't two. The first stage being the basic batch manufacturing environment that is the platform from which you move.

There are six stages in the lean journey.

FAUST: When Freudenberg-NOK began its lean journey in 1992 we were organized by process so all of our molding equipment was in one department or room. We would mold product in a large batch, maybe

50,000 or 100,000 pieces in a batch, then we'd transport that batch to a work-in-process inventory crib, where later a scheduler would take it out and send it to the finishing department. There, those parts would be trimmed and sprung and finally 100 percent inspected to separate the good ones from the bad ones.

The defects in this process were typically generated during molding, so they were not caught until much later. This drives up the risk of high scrap in a batch process. Finally, the good parts were audited by quality control, sent to a packaging area and shipped.

In this kind of arrangement, we produced 5,880 parts per shift, with 46 labor hours per day, with 36,000 pieces of work-in-process inventory. The parts would travel 2,214 feet. The scrap rate was nearly 7 percent. And the lead-time — the time it took for the material to be transformed into a part and get through the system — was typically 30 days. Our productivity was measured as 383 pieces per labor hour.

Stage One is the baseline for the product family.

This arrangement identified in Stage One became the baseline for this product family. This baseline becomes the stake in the ground and the springboard for improvement activity.

DAY: The second stage is the very early efforts being conducted by a lot of companies in the industry, which is pretty embarrassing. In this stage, they learn something about lean, they're not quite sure of what it means and how to do it, but they take some of the practices and they polish up their batch process.

FAUST: In Stage Two, we conducted our initial kaizen project and moved to more of a cellular environment. But at this stage we were really using lean tools to improve a batch operation. Here, the finishing operations were put in closer proximity to the molding press. Our pieces-per-shift jumped up to 6,060. Our labor-hours-per-day were reduced from 46 to 34. Our work-in-process inventory was reduced by 50 percent. And the distance traveled went from 2,200 feet to 670.

We also had a significant impact on scrap, reducing it from 6.8 percent to 4.1 percent. Our lead-time was slashed from 30 days to 20, and our productivity measure went from 383 pieces per labor hour to 534.

Overall, Stage Two resulted in a modest improvement in capacity output, a pretty significant reduction in labor costs, a modest reduction in overhead and a substantial reduction on working capital required.

We were generating savings through those kaizen events, but there was no focus on systems.

In Stage Two, we were using a "low-hanging fruit approach." We were just trying to find the greatest area of opportunity: do a kaizen on that area and then move on to the next greatest area of opportunity. We were generating savings through those kaizen events, but there was no focus on systems.

DAY: The third stage is when you actually break down the batch process and start practicing U-shaped cell, one-piece flow.

All these improvements came just from moving the finishing operations in closer proximity to the molding operation.

That fourth stage is where you get at the overhead cost reduction.

FAUST: In Stage Three, or the model cell phase, we started thinking about the production system. We conducted another kaizen and put all of the value-added steps for this product into a one-piece flow, U-shaped cell. The impact on performance from this step was profound. Our pieces per shift jumped to 6,840. Our labor hours per day dropped from 34 to 24. Our work-in-process inventory fell dramatically from 18,000 to 240 pieces. The distance traveled dropped from 670 to 20 feet. Our scrap rate was slashed from 4.1 percent to 1.3 percent. Our lead-time was slashed from 20 days to just five. And our productivity increased from 534 to 855 pieces per labor hour. All these improvements came just from moving the finishing operations in closer proximity to the molding operation, in terms of both distance and time.

DAY: Those three stages represent the opportunity for variable cost elimination. The real hard costs start to fall out of the system. If you run a project, you'll save money, I can absolutely guarantee that is going to happen.

You then go to the fourth stage, the process of linking all of these islands of success that have occurred in the factory because someone has put a U-shaped cell in one corner and another someplace else. They say, "This is good stuff so let's link it together and in the linking, let's integrate all the indirect labor, integrate what used to be supervisors and let them be group leaders. Let's convert supervisors from being autocrats to facilitators and let's take a couple of layers of management out."

That fourth stage is where you get at the overhead cost reduction. Production controls, inventory management and purchasing all get integrated in. That's when you come up with things like focused factories.

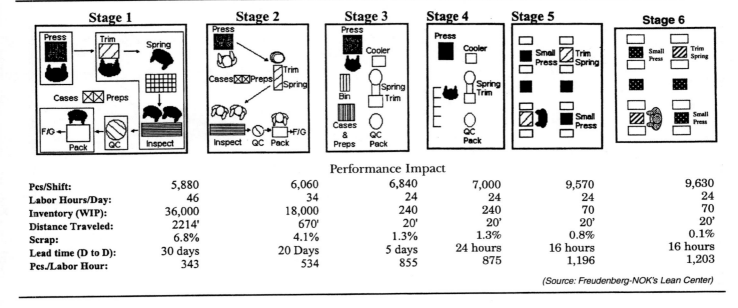

Performance Impact

	Stage 1	Stage 2	Stage 3	Stage 4	Stage 5	Stage 6
Pcs/Shift:	5,880	6,060	6,840	7,000	9,570	9,630
Labor Hours/Day:	46	34	24	24	24	24
Inventory (WIP):	36,000	18,000	240	240	70	70
Distance Traveled:	2214'	670'	20'	20'	20'	20'
Scrap:	6.8%	4.1%	1.3%	1.3%	0.8%	0.1%
Lead time (D to D):	30 days	20 Days	5 days	24 hours	16 hours	16 hours
Pcs./Labor Hour:	343	534	855	875	1,196	1,203

(Source: Freudenberg-NOK's Lean Center)

FAUST: Stage Four represents taking a whole series of model cells created in Stage Three and organizing them on a plant-wide basis into a product focused factory and then developing the appropriate plant-wide support systems for those model cells, such as a plant-wide pull system.

In Stage Four, you have the opportunity to address your overhead costs. For example, when you link model cells in a product-focused factory and create a plant-wide pull system, you eliminate the need for scheduling, expediting and managing work-in-process inventory. It simply evaporates and with it goes at least one and maybe two layers of supervisors or management.

By converting to a focused factory, we made a huge gain in lead-time. While our other measures remained about the same, lead-time dropped from five days to just 24 hours and our overhead fell significantly.

DAY: Stage Five is when you have your focused factory and it's humming along and you ask yourself the hard question, what's next? The next thing is to figure out how to have significant breakthroughs in cost. In other words, let's stop trying to tweak 2 percent or 3 percent out of our cost structure. Is there a better way to do this that might result in a 20 percent reduction?

That's the production preparation process (3-P) phase. That is when you take white sheets and do the gap analysis. But most important, you go through the seven alternatives of producing the value-added steps and you come up with enormous breakthroughs in the cost range of 20 to 40 percent and reductions in capital requirements for equivalent production of 30 to 50 percent.

We're in that stage right now. We're converting old processes with brand new process methods and having enormous reductions in capital and people costs.

FAUST: In Stage Five, the 3-P led to dramatic improvements over and above everything we had accomplished so far. Instead of one large press, we [installed] four smaller presses and we organized all that into essentially the same footprint with the cell still running with the same operator.

3-P was used to obsolete and replace an existing press with a new one to achieve a breakthrough improvement in cost. In our cell's performance, our pieces per shift jumped from 7,000 to 9,570. Work-in-process inventory further dropped from 240 to 70 and scrap declined from 1.3 percent to 0.8 percent, reflecting the improved capability of the smaller presses. Lead-time was cut by a third, to 16 hours. Productivity jumped from 875 to 1,196 pieces per labor hour.

Overall, 3-P had substantial impact on our ability to generate additional revenue, reduce labor cost, cut overhead and decrease working capital for this product. The capital investment cost for the same output dropped about 38 percent. The total manufacturing cost declined about

By converting to a focused factory, we made a huge gain in lead-time.

3-P led to dramatic improvements over and above everything we had accomplished so far.

28 percent. This is another example of real purging of costs, not just shifting cost savings to the next tier.

We have dozens and dozens of 3-P projects throughout Freudenberg-NOK, [an example of which is the] use of 3-P when [we] added capacity for existing products. The original or baseline plan called for a capital investment of $3 million. After 3-P, capital was reduced to $1.7 million. The original plan estimated manufacturing costs of $1.08; with 3-P, this cost was reduced to 78 cents. Labor was reduced from 30 people to 13.

Keep in mind, 3-P was done on an existing product and this existing process was already a highly refined, well-managed process. Yet 3P reduced manufacturing cost by almost 30 percent and cut labor 56 percent. This has now been in production for over two years.

In every case where we've practiced 3-P, even in Freudenberg-NOK's already lean environment, capital was cut more than 40 percent, manufacturing cost was reduced more than 20 percent and labor content fell more than 50 percent. Now you can see why Toyota doesn't want to talk about it! It's the ultimate weapon in their system.

DAY: The sixth stage is to integrate Six Sigma into that lean environment.

FAUST: Six Sigma has been a home run in terms of complementing our lean practices. Stage Six shows the impact of Six Sigma as we introduced that tool into our new 3-P cell. The most significant impact of Six Sigma was in the reduction of defects. Six Sigma practices helped us cut scrap from eight-tenths of a percent, already a respectable level by traditional standards, down to one-tenth of one percent.

If everyone gets to level six, will consumers be ordering cars off the Internet and having them delivered in 15 days?

DAY: That's not my vision. Why are people talking about, "Oh let's build a car in 15 days and deliver it" when they can't make a car and make money? Management's focus is always on the future as opposed to fixing the present situation. How can you get to a 15-day car if you can't make a car that makes money?

What do you do as a CEO on a day-to-day basis to make sure your company progresses down the lean path?

DAY: As an integral part of my business operating system at my level, my staff has to report on lean and Six Sigma performance every month: what gains have been realized; what projects have been completed; and so on. Secondly, we have a certification program and I have a pool of talent that is constantly moving through that certification process. We have informal policies inside the company that our future management talent can only emerge from individuals who have achieved a certain certification level in both lean and Six Sigma. That causes the program to continue to prosper because people know that if they're going to make it to the

Six Sigma has been a home run.

top or make it close to the top, they have to be well versed and knowledgeable and capable of practicing all of the things we talk about. Then our mission statement says pointedly that the basic culture of this company is built on the continuous improvement process.

Is lean an overriding focus in your daily routine?

DAY: I probably spend more than 25 percent of my working day satisfying my curiosity that the processes are proceeding the way they should. When we launched I was up over 40 percent.

What is a big barrier that must be overcome?

DAY: It's the middle management group — those people who spent their lives being autocrats. That's the biggest barrier that exists. The issue there is all about training and exposure. You can't ask someone to stop being an autocrat and start being a facilitator if you don't teach them how to do it.

That was probably our most energy consuming effort. It's not the direct worker that's the issue; it's the person he works for. If you focus properly on getting those people trained and equipped to be good facilitators the process moves much more quickly.

You need a sensei.

What's the important first step a company should take?

DAY: You need a sensei.

How good are Shingijutsu and TBM Consulting?

DAY: They're very, very good at it but keep in mind, they get it off by running successful projects. They don't get it off by teaching others how to do it. That to me is the weakness in their process. I call them drive-by kaizens. They come in and storm the plant, they spend a week and save you gobs of money and then they're out the door and you say, "Jesus, what just happened?" And then the process stops because they didn't leave behind the trained people who could continue the practice. That is what makes the Lean Center different. Our principle objective is to teach, and oh by the way you're going to save enough money along the way to more than pay the cost to learn.

How different is lean from Six Sigma?

DAY: They are clearly complimentary. You can do one or the other or you can do them both; it doesn't really matter. I would tell you the Six Sigma process inside my company is a marvelous, marvelous waste elimination tool and it gets at all the systemic stuff that lean can't get to.

Can you start with Six Sigma and get to lean or is it better to go the other way?

DAY: Absolutely you can. You can go either way. It doesn't matter so long as you have a commitment to do it.

EXIDE TECHNOLOGIES

Exide Technologies, the world's largest manufacturer of batteries with operations in 89 countries and 18,000 employees, is beginning to emerge from the "stone ages" of manufacturing. It is basing its resurrection on an entirely new senior management staff, and a philosophy that embraces and deploys lean tools and techniques.

The company is coming through some troubled times. It was delisted from the New York Stock Exchange in early 2002 and pleaded guilty to fraud charges concerning its relations with Sears and settled with the U.S. Attorney for $27.5 million.

To help extract it from its troubled and tainted past, the company named one of Detroit's industrial icons to chair its board: Robert Lutz, vice chairman of Chrysler Corp.

Lutz's drive to restructure the 113-year-old Princeton, N.J., battery maker started when he hired Craig Muhlhauser from his position as president of Ford's $19-billion Visteon subsidiary to become the chief executive officer. Muhlhauser worked for Pratt & Whitney in the '90s and had been involved in that company's restructuring based upon a lean production model.

Exide was a traditional manufacturing company having difficulties with all aspects of its business. It was unable to attract investment for new product development; not able to meet commitments to employees, customers or suppliers; and struggling to meet its environmental responsibilities, which were substantial.

Lean production was viewed as the only viable option to save the firm, so Lutz and Muhlhauser hired Robert Weiner from Pratt & Whitney to implement a strategy.

Weiner, Exide's senior vice president for global manufacturing and engineering, developed a program called EXCELL — Exide Customer-focused Excellence Lean Leadership — that would be deployed simultaneously across 60 Exide facilities around the globe. The idea is to eliminate waste and implement continuous flow and customer pull throughout the company's supply chain. The company hopes to double the output of its facilities with existing space and people and improve its cost of quality by two times by 2005.

The company has set interim goals for its various plants that it calls "Copper," a plant's first level of achievement that improves dock-to-dock time, days of on-hand inventory, build-to-schedule rates, blood lead levels in workers, accidents, lost time incidents and quality. The next levels of achievement under EXCELL are Bronze, Silver, Gold and Platinum. When a plant achieves the "Platinum" level, it means it has deployed a one-piece flow system where errors are impossible; machine uptime is 99.9 percent; it has self-operating shop floors; no accidents; the lowest employee turnover rate; and the highest level of customer satisfaction.

It took about five or six years before it really became a way of life.

Is the lean transformation you're undertaking at Exide different from the lean transformation at Pratt & Whitney?

WEINER: When we started lean in 1994, Pratt was losing $300 million a year. When I left they were making $1.2 billion. Every year, you didn't recognize the lean system going in because we made so many changes to it. It took about five or six years before it really became a way of life.

We started the effort with Shingijutsu along with [Yuzuru] Ito who had a great quality system called QCPC — quality control process charting. Ito and I put that in place at Pratt in 1994 while at the same time we were doing kaizen events. The two were very different because Shingijutsu is flow and takt time and quality is usually last in their minds.

Ito didn't like Shingijutsu and in his mind quality was everything. He believed that if you fixed quality the flow would be there. In reality you need both. We worked both of those for several years and installed a process in 1995 that incorporated both that we called ACE — Achieving Competitive Excellence, which was five levels of lean. ACE is now across all of UTC [United Technologies Corp.] in every division.

Is your EXCELL program the same as ACE?
WEINER: The big difference between ACE and EXCELL is that EXCELL is tied to metrics. For instance, as part of achieving the first level of lean, we want our plants to [implement] total productive maintenance on their toughest 10 percent of their machines and improve uptime by 10 percent. We forced that requirement on the highest constraint equipment. Our metrics for achieving the first level of lean varied by plant, but we also required improvements in productivity by up to 20 percent and 20 percent reductions in scrap. When you have those metrics you end up with results.

It started both at Pratt and at Exide as a significant emotional event, but we have an even bigger emotional event here than we did at Pratt. Pratt lost a lot of money when we started it but Pratt was UTC. Exide was losing lots of money when we started it, but Exide doesn't have a UTC structure behind it.

Is it true that the only way companies start a lean transformation is if they are under threat of bankruptcy?
WEINER: That was the case at Exide. We told the employees that we have an option: we're either going to do something dramatic and turn the company around or go out of business. People rally behind that. You have to get the message out so they understand you're serious and that this isn't just the corporate office saying something that is not true. You rally everybody behind a significant emotional event.

Did you tell Exide's employees that it is a significant emotional event?
WEINER: While I call it a significant emotional event, I tell them it's survival. Either we become lean or we're out of business.

Our biggest competitor in the battery business is Johnson Controls. They started lean about six years ago and they continue to produce more batteries in existing facilities, which continues to drive costs down and their pricing down.

This is the opposite of what we were doing. We were continuing to add more capacity. Eventually you run out of runway and get to the point where you can't compete any more. I don't think we would have made it another year.

Beyond lean is there another system that could be put in place to save an old-line manufacturing company like Exide?
WEINER: Lean is the only system to do it, because you have a real manufacturing company here that is going to either take costs out or not

It started as a significant emotional event.

I don't think we would have made it another year.

be here. The only other way to do it is to become a marketing company and sell all the plants and contract your manufacturing.

That is a strategy many companies are adopting.
WEINER: We're looking at all the different options, too. Do we want to be so vertically integrated? We're the most vertically integrated company I've seen. We make our own plastics and our own lead. The only thing we don't do is go to the mines and take the ore out. We make batteries and we pick them back up when the customer is finished using them. We reuse the lead and reuse the plastic. It's an expensive proposition. When you have a smelter that makes lead that has been there for 50 years it requires a lot of capital and it's a huge environmental issue. We continue to upgrade the facilities in order to stay ahead of the environmental game. We're looking at different strategies, like do we want to stay in the smelter game and do we want to continue making plastics. What we want to make is batteries.

At Pratt, we got out of virtually everything other than producing the engine and the highly technical components that go into it — everything else was outsourced. We're looking at the same thing here.

There are still many companies that are debating whether lean is the thing to do in order for them to stay alive. What do you think?
WEINER: I think anybody who doesn't believe that lean is the solution will eventually put themselves out of business. You don't realize it until you start it. I was in a number of our plants in the last couple of weeks because we are doing our first awards, which is the "Copper" award for the first level of achievement. I was in Kansas City for the first plant that has achieved Copper and what they've done in such a short period of time is just unbelievable.

Remember, these are employees who knew nothing about lean eight months ago. This was the first plant I brought Shingijutsu in and at the end of the first week of a kaizen event, they built a new prototype of an assembly line and two of these new assembly lines are in production today. The U-shaped line they have now has almost half the people than the one they had before. Quality issues are almost gone. There is no inventory on the line. It's a complete pull system and they have a kanban system set up where instead of having the suppliers delivering the product to a receiving dock and going into an inventory area and onto a shelf, that whole inventory area is gone and the supplier delivers right to the line. Our supply base now delivers every day.

To have these people take you around and show you this is so exciting. One guy showed me his equipment on which we did a TPM event. It's the most critical equipment in the plant where we make lead strips and it runs 24 hours a day, seven days a week, 365 days a year. It was running around 82 percent on time, today it runs at 94 percent. They were so excited to show me what they had done. They have plexiglass in front

Anybody who doesn't believe lean is the solution will put themselves out of business.

It's just unbelievable how much can be done in such a short amount of time.

of it instead of cabinets that you couldn't see through. Now you can look inside. They have gauges that you can see. We have green, yellow and red ranges on the gauges. They have check lists. At the beginning of every shift the operators walk through the check list. It's just unbelievable how much can be done in such a short amount of time.

Then I was in Castanheira in Portugal last week at our second plant in Europe to get Copper. As diverse a culture as Portugal is, it wasn't a lot different than the enthusiasm I saw at Kansas City. I just couldn't believe the amount of change a plant did in such a short period of time.

Many companies take five or six years to instill this into their culture. Is it possible to kaizen a culture over night?

WEINER: When I was interviewed by Bob Lutz for this job a little over a year ago he and [Exide CEO] Craig [Muhlhauser] wanted me to implement lean across the company. Bob said to me, "My recommendation is to take one of our big plants and implement lean over there, make it the best in the world and then we'll take what we learned there and we'll put it in all of our other plants." I said, "Bob, you don't have time to do that. If you did that it would take you two years at best to get that plant where you wanted it to be, and probably three years and then you start your other plants. It will be another three to five years and by then you'll be out of business. You need to do them all."

He said, "That's impossible. You can't do them all because we have 62 plants around the world and 62 cultures. It will never work."

I said, "Bob, we'll do it."

Is it possible to do them all at once?

WEINER: You have to have a real system in place with a core organization capable of doing it all. I had to narrow it down a little bit to tier-one, tier-two and tier-three plants, with tier one being our top 25 plants and tier two being our next group. Plants I'm not worrying about are in tier three because we're in the process of selling or getting out of those businesses.

In eight months all of the tier-one and just about all the tier-two plants are at the new operations culture. Don't think we didn't have to change plant managers and a whole bunch of people, but I can't even believe how much excitement the plant people have.

Don't think we didn't have to change plant managers.

How did you go about making the change?

WEINER: It started at the top with Bob Lutz and Craig Muhlhauser saying that we're going to put this in the company and Bob is going to make it happen. We had a top-100 management meeting in Orlando last May where I rolled it out. In rolling it out, I talked about the system and the benefits and a lot of people nodded their heads and said, "Yeah, yeah, yeah, I've heard this before."

But I had put a core organization in place with a head of lean. We

We had massive training.

hired six lean agents some who were experts in lean and others who were internal people that we felt were capable of being experts in lean. Then we put a lean leader in every plant. In most cases, we went to the plant and hand-picked somebody in the plant who was bright-eyed, bushy-tailed and really loved the concept and was close with the people, as opposed to going out and hiring someone with a lot of experience at it.

Then we had massive training.

I had zero people who knew lean when we started. I hired a head of lean who knew lean, so now we had two out of 18,000 people in the company.

Did you hire outside consultants?

WEINER: We hired a number of people who left Pratt's Office of Continuous Improvement to form their own lean consulting companies. I brought on board Tom DeForge and we put a complete lean system together which incorporated the Pratt ACE process and what we learned from Ito. We put a very detailed training program together and in August we brought all of the lean leaders we had just put in place in every plant in for week-long training sessions on lean. The following week we did the same thing in Europe.

Then I brought Shingijutsu on board and we started doing kaizen events. Tom DeForge and his group were doing at least two kaizen events a week in different plants and we cross-pollinated the effort. We'd do a kaizen event in Kansas City but in doing the kaizen event, the requirement was lean leaders and other people from every plant had to be part of that kaizen event. Every plant within that business segment had to send two people to Kansas City's kaizen event. We had 30 at the event and probably 18 of them were from outside the plant. Then we did other kaizen events at other locations and did the same cross pollination. We went to another location with all different people.

When we were training the plant on a kaizen event, we'd have seven or eight other plants involved. Then we'd go to another plant and do the same thing. Before you know it after having done 30 or 40 kaizen events in a couple of months, you now have 40 to 60 people from every plant that have been involved in it. They all learn from each other. They went back and did their own kaizens. Then I did a total productive maintenance event at a plant in the same way

Each lean leader and the top management at every plant had to have 160 hours of training — 40 hours of lean training, 80 hours of kaizen event participation and 40 hours of a TPM event. The employees below that have either participated in kaizen events, are part of a TPM event or are part of something within the plant, which is the QCPC.

It builds upon itself.

Now what happens is it builds upon itself because when you do a kaizen event, you say wow, look at what I've done in a week, this is unbelievable, and they want to go out and do more and more and more. For example, in our Bristol [Tenn.] facility, the second biggest battery plant in

These people are so excited.

the world, they had 16 assembly lines where they made 900 batteries per line per shift. They had requested about a year ago to buy $3 million in equipment to put another assembly line in. We did a kaizen event there and we found that we can actually produce almost 1,900 batteries per shift per line. We cancelled the equipment. We've now doubled the capacity of the assembly line and have shut down most of our third shift operation because we don't need it. These people are so excited.

We did the same thing in our Salina [Kansas] plant, which is the largest battery plant in the world. Based on what they have done there, the plan for this year is their volume will go up 25 percent, their head count will be down by 5 percent; they'll have a 32 percent increase in productivity and the cost per battery will go down 9 percent. That is the biggest battery plant in the world. I get so excited when I talk about this.

Do the people who run a process that is producing 900 batteries per line per shift realize that they can be running at 1,800 batteries overnight?

WEINER: They realize it and you know what's interesting is they said I worked harder at 900 per shift than I do at 1,800 per shift. I stood there and watched them when we were doing 900. It's like five chickens running around. They run from one end of the line to the other and we get a backlog at one machine and then they run down and put them on a skid and run away and the fork truck driver didn't take the skid away and the line stops and they run up to the other end of the line. You have five people running around.

They changed it to making a battery every 30 seconds and in doing that they set up takt time. Someone making a battery at 18 seconds was pushing it to a guy who could only do it in 30 seconds and all he did was back up the second guy. The first guy worked hard and stopped, worked hard and stopped. So we slowed the whole line down to run at 30 seconds and everyone worked at a pace. Then we put lights at the end of the line so that when a skid filled up, the fork truck driver would come and take away the pallet. The answer from everyone on that line is that they are not working as hard as they were before.

They're not working any harder but are making more money.

The other thing that got them excited is that plant has an incentive plan. If you have five people on a line making 900 batteries and you have the same five people on the line making 1,800 batteries, they're excited because they're not working any harder but are making more money.

What does the old plant manager say when he comes in and sees this radical improvement? Does he say what was wrong with me? Was I a bonehead?

WEINER: In our Fort Smith [Ark.] plant, we had a plant manager who said it indirectly that he didn't buy any of this stuff. "I've been a battery man for 35 years and this is a bunch of hogwash." That was a plant that didn't go anywhere and four months later we changed the plant manager. Today, it's one of our best plants. You have plant managers like that. You have other plant managers who say, "Wow, this really works."

What we have tried to do is not criticize people for not seeing this, but reward them for doing it. They've looked at it and taken off with it.

What are some of the rewards you've put in place?
WEINER: When most people do this, they pick a certain level of performance and require that their people achieve that number. What we did with our "Copper" requirement is we didn't have any plants competing with each other. We took baselines for everybody. If you were delivering your product 70 percent on time and another plant was 95 percent on time, to get Copper, the one that was doing 70 percent had to get to 85 percent — halfway to 100 — and the plant at 95 percent had to get to 97.5 percent. We rewarded both the same. We kept the competition to get the "Copper" level but not to have better numbers than competing plants.

Were many of the plant managers cognizant of lean? Had they started to hear about it?
WEINER: Bob Lutz said to me that Exide was like a company that had taken all the people, put them in a submarine, and stayed underwater for about 20 years and just surfaced. Not a lot of people were cognizant of it.

Even though Johnson Controls was zooming forward?
WEINER: They knew that, but they didn't understand what they did to be successful.

The neat thing about lean is that it's basic manufacturing that is common sense. If you come across to people that this is common sense, you can see the benefit and it's something you've known for 20 or 30 years, but all we're doing is putting in a structured approach to implementing it.

What's bad is bringing in a bunch of consultants who immediately begin to say you guys don't know what you're doing, let me show you a better way. We didn't do any of that. I'm a manufacturing guy, I'm not a consultant, so we go in and say, "This makes sense." We did it very much in a coaching environment.

Most everybody bought in. I needed a lot of soldiers with me; my head of manufacturing for North America and Europe — to be totally bought in. We needed to change a few of them, but we got the best and they became my spokesmen and they were driving it as hard as anybody. They are fanatics about it now.

Is there a good pool of people to select from?
WEINER: I didn't hire that many people other than some lean experts; a head of lean. But all my plant managers, my heads of manufacturing, though I removed a bunch of them, we got people from within the business.

Lean is basic manufacturing that is common sense.

Did Shingijutsu put a lot of people on this?

WEINER: For the first six months, we did, but I backed them down. I had three groups doing kaizen events: Shingijutsu, JDI, which is Tom DeForge from Pratt, and Jeff Wagner also from Pratt. What happened is Shingijutsu is three-and-a-half times more expensive than the other guys. They're about $35,000 for a week. They were so driven in terms of getting results that I'm not sure the benefits over the long haul were what we needed. Shingijutsu just shakes up a whole plant. We needed it in a few places but then the other guys we were working with turned out to be better.

This year, I essentially stopped Shingijutsu and am doing a few kaizen events with Tom DeForge and Jeff Wagner. But now I have most of the plants doing it themselves and the lean agents I hired from the outside are just as good as anybody in doing a kaizen. I have six of them and they're required to do 10 kaizen events per year per person. So that gives me 60 weeks with them plus our internal ones. So we have weaned ourselves off of the consultants.

This year, the main purpose of the Tom DeForge group is to teach. So now we have a one-week training on "Bronze," which is our second level. This is more detailed into the pull system, kanban and TPM. We are now sending everyone through 40 hours of training for the second level.

The other thing we're doing is business process reengineering events. We started that three months ago because you can't just do manufacturing without fixing your system. We've done BPR events in logistics, accounts payable and we're starting to set up the same process with our salaried organization with the same criteria and the same levels. We're just now putting that group together and we're sending our salaried workers through 40 hours of BPR training.

Isn't lean for HR and accounting tougher than the lean for manufacturing?

WEINER: All of a sudden you have a great process in place, you have a pull system with the suppliers and you're pulling it through the plant, but you find you have no forecasting system with your customers because your system doesn't operate right or you can't pay your bills or your suppliers have no idea what they need to deliver to you because they have no visibility on your sales. What happens is six months into it your new constraint is your white collar. Now we're having a lot of BPR [business process reengineering] events and that is the routine.

Does 5-S work its way into the office environment?

WEINER: In the Princeton office, we're getting everyone to turn on 5-S in the office. You go into some of the offices in Princeton and you can't even see the person behind the desk. If you look at some of our maintenance mechanics or operators who look for a tool to do a set up and you open the tool box and there are hundreds of tools sitting in there

Shingijutsu just shakes up a whole plant.

Six months into it, your new constraint is your white collar.

and they spend hundreds of hours looking for a tool. You take that and create a shadow board where they know where everything is. There is no difference between that and a salaried person. You can spend an hour looking for a piece of paper or you can organize it, but they are a little bit more stubborn and it takes more work.

Do you force your salaried people to do it?
WEINER: In our accounts payable group, we did a BPR event and we couldn't get organized. There was no good system for paying people. We did an event there and we found that the person who was running the organization was not in tune to make a change, so we replaced him. It will be the exact same approach.

Do you need a moniker like EXCELL in order for lean to work?
WEINER: You have to because if you walk into any plant right now, you'll see the big logo everywhere. You see it in the lobby and offices in the plant. Everyone talks and says "Copper," which is the first level of EXCELL. In a very short period of time it becomes the word people use to become the best. To get the Copper Award in such a short period of time is such an achievement for a plant, and they are proud of that.

Were you surprised by the condition of the plants when you started there?
WEINER: It was like the stone ages of manufacturing. But there was so much opportunity that it was more than proverbial low-hanging fruit. The fruit was hitting me in the head as we were walking through the plants. I told the management meeting that the opportunities are just huge and think of where we'll be when we capitalize on them.

How hard is it to see this materialize on the bottom line? Do you see financial results you can point to as easily as you can point to an improved process?
WEINER: You have to do two things with lean. You can lean out a facility, take all the costs out, but that is not enough because what's happening is we're taking the costs out and we're able to combine plants. We have an industrial plant in Kankakee [Ill.] and we have another network power plant in Fort Smith. We are closing the Kankakee plant and moving all the work to our Fort Smith plant. We couldn't have done this without lean. We are doubling the volume in the Fort Smith plant. We're taking 220 people's worth of work at Kankakee and we're doing it with 80 at Fort Smith and we'll end up with 40 when we're done. So we've doubled the capacity of a plant and ultimately save $1 million a month. That is the bottom line. The problem is we'll have a plant up in Kankakee that we can't sell. It's going to be sitting there idle.

But the second part of lean that you have to do is the reason you do lean. What do you do after you drive your costs down, increase your

Exide was like the stone ages of manufacturing.

capacity, improve your quality and eliminate waste? More sales. If I can take any plant and go from 900 units per shift to 1,800 units per shift, the solution is to bring in more business, and you can do it for no cost other than the material cost of the product. That is better than anybody can do in the market. We'll see dramatic things this year with costs coming out, but the real dramatic aspect is when you bring in new sales.

Can you describe Ito's quality system?

WEINER: He was [UTC CEO] George David's right-hand guy. So when Ito visited a plant you were either ready or gone because the fear was just phenomenal. I was like a translator for him trying to get people to understand what he was really saying, which was quality is everything. If you eliminate all quality defects you will have really fixed your whole manufacturing system. So let's put quality first.

Putting quality first means that you will do whatever it takes to mistake-proof every quality defect that you have and if you do that, you will have fixed your whole system. You have to literally say that no matter what your quality defect is you will come up with a way to mistake proof it so that it will be gone forever. If that means you have to change the design, if that means you have to change the suppliers' design, if that means you have to change the way you manufacture the product, you will do that because you will spare no expense in eliminating that quality defect. That is the one big difference between Ito and any other quality system.

With any other quality system, you say, "Let me do a cost justification for eliminating that quality defect." If you say it cost more to make that engineering change than it would be for what I save on the quality cost, then the difference is you don't do it. With Ito, you do whatever it takes to eliminate the quality defect. That changes the whole psychology of the company because you say, "I don't care what it cost to fix that problem. I will not accept any quality defects in my company." That was a big difference.

What are the foundations of the Quality Control Process Charting system?

WEINER: We map out every element in the process. Everything in the process that is different from the standard way in which you build it is called a turnback. For instance, in the battery industry, if you have a person putting plugs on top of a battery and they pull a lever down and squeeze it into the top, if one of the plugs doesn't get squeezed down and you have to pull a rubber mallet out and bang it in, that is called a turnback. We add up all the turnbacks on the line and we determine a turnback ratio.

When you do this, you typically come back with a ratio of 800 or 1,000 percent or even 1,500 percent, which means that everything you build gets reworked 15 times in the line. When you realize that, everyone

The real dramatic aspect is when you bring in new sales.

"I will not accept any quality defects in my company."

says, "Wow, that's pretty startling."

Now you collect all this data and you simply pareto the top three; and you take three months and you mistake-proof it. You make them disappear. Then you do the next three and mistake-proof those. If you are relentless and truly eliminate the problem, in six months you will have reduced those turnbacks by 50 percent and at the end of one year, you reduce them by 90 percent. It happens every time.

The 1,500 percent turns into 150 percent in a year and then a year later it turns into 15 percent and then a year later it turns into 1.5 percent. That is the process.

The mistake-proofing portion is the most difficult because you have to use techniques to determine the root cause.

You have to get the data, but the mistake-proofing portion is the most difficult because you have to use techniques to determine the root cause. Then you have to go and implement it with engineering or a process on the line.

Projected Results of EXCELL

- No waste
- One-piece flow
- Pure Value Add
- Errors Are Impossible
- Optimized Process Time
- Beyond Six Sigma in Quality
- Machine Uptime is at 99.96 Percent
- Inventory is Maintained by Suppliers
- Solid, Trustworthy Partnerships With Suppliers
- Defect-Free, 100 Percent On-Time Deliveries to Customers
- Total Involvement of All Employees in Decisions
- Highest Flexibility to Meet Customer Demand
- The Benchmark for All Manufacturers
- Lowest Cost Producer of Batteries
- Entire Organization is Integrated
- Highest Customer Satisfaction
- Self-Operating Shop Floor
- Lowest Turnover Rate
- Accident Free

HON INDUSTRIES / SIMPLER

One of the earliest American converts to the lean production system that originated in Japan was George Koenigsaecker, who eventually deployed the technique at Jake Brake where he was president in the late 1980s. At the time, the concept was not known as lean, but as just-in-time production, developed by Taiichi Ohno and a small team of zealots at Toyota. Koenigsaecker's work at Jake Brake formed the foundation of what became the Danaher Business System, one of the most successful lean implementations in the world.

In the 1990s, Koenigsaecker deployed lean at office furniture maker HON Industries, also with great success.

Koenigsaecker is now in charge of business development with Simpler, a lean consulting firm based in Ottumwa, Iowa. He is also chairman of the Shingo Prize for Excellence in Manufacturing, which is awarded every year to companies adopting lean production techniques. It is named in honor of Shigeo Shingo, one of the Japanese developers of lean principles.

The more experience you have in manufacturing, the harder it is to do lean.

A lean enterprise conversion is something that takes about a decade.

Why is it taking so long for lean production to take root in the United States?

KOENIGSAECKER: The hard part of implementing lean isn't so much that it's intellectually difficult; it's that there are a bunch of key principles that are fundamentally opposite of the way you do things in mass or batch production. The more experience you have in manufacturing, the harder it is to do lean.

When we started in the late 1980s, it was very experimental. Even today, leaving out the organizations like Toyota and some of its suppliers that brought the system with them, there are very few organizations that have stuck to it long enough really to show the potential of what is properly called a lean enterprise, where they have applied it throughout production and the administrative sides of the business.

Why have so few companies adopted lean?

KOENIGSAECKER: Part of it is the program-of-the-year phenomenon. There is also the problem that whenever there is a new CEO or a division president, they feel they have to put their mark on things, which is typically a two- or three-year phenomenon. A lean enterprise conversion is something that takes about a decade. The good news is that every year you make significant progress in cost, quality and delivery. But to become really lean is a very long journey.

Jake Brake today is approaching lean. They are making 4.8 times as many engine brakes per hour than they were a decade ago — a 480 percent output increase. That is the kind of metric that is possible with a full-scale lean conversion.

What are some of the difficulties in starting a conversion away from batch and queue to flow manufacturing?

KOENIGSAECKER: We have a mindset that if you apply a tool, you've done it and you're done. So we go in and build cells, apply standard work and typically get on each pass a 40 percent productivity gain. But to get the 400 percent gain you have to pass it at least 10 different

This is a counter-intuitive thing.

"Wow, if they could do that we can be in big trouble."

times. You must restudy the process over and over.

That is a counter-intuitive thing. People say the words continuous improvement, but we just don't believe in continuous improvement. The idea that you can take a series of tools and apply them again and again to the same area and every time you apply them you find new levels of waste and new ways to improve doesn't feel right.

If you take 10 firms that started on lean, eight of them quit after the first pass because they got a significant improvement of 40 percent. They thought that was the end of the journey. It's a small number that have actually learned the lesson that if you keep applying the tools the gains keep coming.

What compelled you to adopt a lean system of production in the late 1980s at Jake Brake when it was a concept that was hardly known in the United States?

KOENIGSAECKER: In the mid '70s, I was in Japan working for Deere & Co. and one of the things we were doing was setting up a business relationship with Yanmar Diesel, which made farm tractors used in Japan. I was one of the people in charge of setting up this relationship. It was an important deal to Yanmar because they were just coming off the early '70s oil crisis that hit Japan really hard.

In one of the management review meetings with the whole senior staff of the company, they went through the improvement they made on a firm-wide basis in three years and they described a doubling of output per person and a reduction in average unit costs of 28 percent.

At the same time, they were producing four times as many product models because they were trying to grow their way out of the recession with proliferation. So their job got four times as hard but they got twice as productive and reduced their unit costs by 28 percent. That was just mind-boggling to me as a manufacturing guy. It caught my attention. I thought, "Wow, if they could do that we can be in big trouble."

I found that they were a loose cousin with the Toyota group of companies and Taiichi Ohno, who had developed the Toyota Production System, had been visiting them every once in a while saying, "You ought to try this new production system we're developing."

They would say, "That sounds interesting but we're happy. See you later."

When the oil crisis just about sunk them, they decided to try it. What I had seen while I was there was three years of weekend work by Ohno and a couple of guys from the Autonomous Study Group, which was a group of internal Toyota and Toyota subsidiary people that Ohno selected to help him develop the system.

Later in the 1980s, I moved to Rockwell International's Automotive Group in Detroit and was able to lead a multiyear benchmarking effort. I was still very intrigued by what I had seen at Yanmar and was trying to understand how it worked and I figured the automotive industry would be closer to it than anybody else. We benchmarked 144 manufacturing firms in Japan and what we found was that 25 percent of them operated on a totally different planetary system from what we were used to.

Rockwell Automotive was a producer of heavy truck components and was usually number one or number two in North American market share in every product we made. We thought we were a pretty good benchmark. We found firms making identical products that were running at 400 percent of our productivity level and 10 times our inventory turns and one-tenth our defect rates. There were huge, order-of-magnitude differences.

One of the shocks for us was that they weren't just four times as productive in the factory. As we double checked, we found that they were on average four times more productive in all the staff departments when you measured in terms of company sales per person in the finance department. That really reaffirmed the magnitude of what I had seen at Yanmar, which wasn't even lean yet.

I began to realize that the nugget of a lean enterprise was the Toyota Production System and its evolution into being a business system that affected the administrative areas and product development and those kinds of functions.

By the time I got to be president of Jake in the late '80s, I was absolutely convinced it was the thing to do from 15 years of studying it from afar. We started doing it at Jake Brake and six months in I ran into three guys who had just retired from Toyota who had all been on this Autonomous Study Group. They became my sensei, or master teachers and so now for the past 15 years, I've been their student on the techniques.

What are some of the key lessons you learned from the ex-Toyota experts?

KOENIGSAECKER: I've learned that learning the techniques take a long time but is only about half the battle. The management of the process has some really unique characteristics that most of the people at Toyota don't realize any more because Ohno fought through those battles 30 years ago. They've forgotten that they had to battle in order to get it in place.

There are some key managerial lessons about implementing this that are still not very well known and still cause almost everyone who embarks on it to run into the same issues because they are inherent with the difference in the process.

What are some of the common problems?

KOENIGSAECKER: Little things like one-piece flow. What you find is people will build a cell and then you'll find batches at each machine within the cell. There are little piles of inventory. The operators feel comfortable with that because that is how they grew up. The supervisors know

Learning the techniques takes a long time but is only about half the battle.

they've always had inventory between the machines. And everybody is afraid to take it out.

I have to admit that after having been a student of this it still took me two years of running and improving cells before I made the leap and actually went to a true one-piece flow.

That then leads to another Toyota philosophy called making the waste visible. It sounds mundane, but it means that the system is designed so that if you implement it but you don't follow up on it, you shut your factory down.

One-piece flow forces the cell to stop functioning until you solve a lot of quality, set up and tool change problems.

It feels so painful, you say this can't be right and yet that's what it is intended to do. The whole idea is to make it so painful to leave all of those problems unresolved that it pushes you to solve those problems.

You're taking two steps backwards to go one step forward. It must be disconcerting.

KOENIGSAECKER: Fundamentally, it just feels wrong both to the production workforce and the management team because they have all been trained in a different system. You go through the whole conversion process and there are a whole bunch of things like that.

What are some others?

KOENIGSAECKER: As a rule of thumb, you should go back to each area at least every other year or once a year if you're on a faster pace and apply all of the tools again and make another round of improvement. This leads you to rethink what sort of organization you need to have if you're going to maintain that sort of improvement pace.

What is the most difficult aspect of managing a conversion?

KOENIGSAECKER: Ohno talked about an organization being like the human body and that a human body is designed to be self protective. There are antibodies inside the body. When a foreign substance enters the body — an infection — the antibodies not only get more active they also multiply. Ohno says an organization operates the same way.

The antibodies create a company's culture. The stronger the culture, the stronger the antibodies because they define what a company will do and also what it won't do.

When you start a conversion like this, you're redefining your company culture in terms of what you will and won't do. The people who are the most loyal members who you know love the company will be some of the biggest resisters of the process because they are trying to protect the company as it has been as opposed to how the company will be. You need to actively address that group or their efforts to protect the corporate culture will defeat any effort to change the culture in a way that will allow you to become a lean enterprise.

Fundamentally, it just feels wrong.

The people who are the most loyal members who you know love the company will be some of the biggest resisters...

If I look at firms that are lean, it's about 3 percent of manufacturing employers in North America...

It takes strong leadership to overcome such resistance to change.
KOENIGSAECKER: And leadership always is in short supply. There is little reward for it and a lot of risk.

Yet you still see many case studies of companies that have adopted lean and experienced dramatic improvements in every measure.
KOENIGSAECKER: If I look at firms that are lean, it's about 3 percent of manufacturing employers in North America and two points of that are transplants like Toyota and its subsidiaries. So it's perhaps 1 percent — and that might even be a stretch. But HON Industries doubled its productivity and tripled its volume in the 90s with the process. Danaher has put it in place in most of its groups and it's pretty well stuck there.

What's the reason behind Danaher's success?
KOENIGSAECKER: Maybe part of it is that they had two young guys who were primary shareholders who were able to latch onto it and consistently support it. This is an interesting phenomenon because they came out of real estate and it probably helped because they didn't know you couldn't do this stuff. When we started doing it, they said it seems logical what you're saying and they didn't know that it was "illogical."

Not even the people at Toyota feel like they have even come close to achieving their goals, and they've been at it for 50 years.
KOENIGSAECKER: The key to doing this is having an attitude that you can always be better tomorrow than you are today. They have these tools and every time they apply them they improve their operation. They are already way out in front because of the attitude that they have a long way to go.

If they're in front now and have been for so long, what happens to Toyota's competitors?
KOENIGSAECKER: It takes a long time for a huge company to erode. I was told about a year ago that Toyota has more cash in the bank than the market capitalization of General Motors. That tells a story. There is a lot of hubris around the old-line former leaders. It's part of the company culture that prevents them from accepting lean because it wasn't something that Sloan developed and it wasn't something that was part of the GM way. There is no one willing to say, "We need to become a new GM." There isn't even the recognition that they need to change. It's absolutely mind-boggling.

What advice do you have for a company that is considering implementing a lean system?
KOENIGSAECKER: You first need to point out to the organization that it needs to change and that staying as it is is a recipe for long-term disaster. The second is to find a good master teacher or sensei to keep you

away from the big roadblocks. Then get a good value-stream based map and plan. The fourth is to build a supportive organizational structure.

We have some rules of thumb that say 3 to 5 percent of the employees at a site should be committed full time to improvement. From our experience it takes about that level of commitment to review every process every two years. We recommend one person at a site be committed and then for every five people you free up reinvest one in the process until you get to that 3 to 5 percent level. Those are the folks you leave to focus on this set of tools until they become your internal sensei.

You need to stick with it for five years and over time, they will touch every part of the organization.

The one thing you see missing from most companies trying to do this is they don't build a structure to sustain it. When you think about it, we are all fighting fires. That is how we manage. We don't do anything that addresses the root cause because that would take time.

You have to take resources and say, "You are not allowed to fight fires, you're only allowed to work full time on root cause improvement projects." If you don't do that, then all of your improvement resources get sucked back into today's fire fighting and you end up not making any fundamental root-cause improvements.

That seems to be the greatest difficulty for any organization. They're all faced with a time crunch, running on a treadmill going 1,000 miles per hour, faster by the day.

KOENIGSAECKER: It's a huge discipline, because when you start, you're all working 12-hour days and you know that if you work a 14-hour day then tomorrow you'll still have the same pile of problems. We're not really driving them out structurally, changing our processes.

When you start off and say you are required as a site manager to assign your best person in the organization to this role of lean development office, that is something that just feels wrong. It's another one of those feel-wrong things. Then when you say for every five people who come out of the events that are freed up, that the lean development office gets to add one more until they become 3 to 5 percent it is just hard to believe. Once you get the people in there, the temptation for most managers is to say, "We have to ship this product today, let's put them on the line today." It takes a rare discipline to get out of the batch production, fire-fighting mode.

I know a $50 million company that is growing and has a great business and it can't ship its products fast enough. If they applied lean it would create capacity that they just can't believe. But they can't get over the hurdle of we're too busy to think about adopting lean. The CEO doesn't have any basis on which to believe that it would be worth the effort to double their capacity in two years by applying lean. Intellectually, you can't convince him while he is sitting there, which is true with all of manufacturing: you have to show people.

Companies trying to do this don't build a structure to sustain it.

It takes a rare discipline to get out of batch production...

How important are outside consultants in the process?

KOENIGSAECKER: There are so many mistakes you can make both on the management, learning and application of the tools themselves that if you don't have a good coach beside you, you're more likely to get shot down than you are to reach the end of the road.

You have to start at a single plant site and pick a product family and use value-stream mapping to look at where the time is wasted and where the value-added and non-value-added steps are in the process. That can give you a map of where to begin in terms of getting results.

When you look at the value-stream map you can see where the non-value adding steps or the time consumption steps are big. With this operational map, you start applying the tools to the subsets within the value stream. You can decide to use Shingo's setup reduction tools to reduce the set up time because that is why things are being held up, or you can put kanban in to link operations. The idea is to get it flowing.

Then the right thing to do is to restudy that value stream again and again so that the organization gets the lesson that, "We made huge improvements but when we went back, it got even better and when we went back again it got even better." You need to sink that logic in early on.

A common format of using these tools that came out of Toyota is to study a small sub segment of one area for a week and make a big improvement. If everyone knows that the goal is to have it be different at the end of one week, it creates a different environment as opposed to, "We're going to analyze it for several months and then do something."

If you count those weeklong periods of applying lean tools to any administrative or production process as a learning experience, it takes 50 or 60 of those before you actually begin to believe in most of the principles. If you can do one of those a month, which is a pretty good pace from following up on the last one and getting ready for the next, you're talking about five or six years before you believe in the basic principles and another three or four years before you are competent at using most of the tools.

Even though you know how to use them, you still may not be willing to put one-piece flow in place. This is why they use the idea of the sensei, which is a martial arts concept. You must have a master teacher and you learn by doing. You don't go to classrooms. You go out and practice the exercise.

Lean is learned the same way. You go out in an environment where your processes are and you apply the tools. It is out of that process that you come to believe the process works.

With the manufacturing sector in a downturn, do you think companies are running out of time to start the process?

KOENIGSAECKER: The good news about the downturn is that more people are willing to seriously look at undertaking a lean journey.

You still may not be willing to put one-piece flow in place.

Wall Street richly rewards the companies that undertake lean but without focusing on it. Why isn't there much pressure from Wall Street to adopt lean?

KOENIGSAECKER: If they went back to Danaher 10 years ago and looked at them as they were then, they would say that is just another dog of an industrial company. But each quarter along the way they look at the cumulative record and they get impressed by the numbers.

I always tell people who are considering the journey that they should just remember that their board of directors is a surrogate for Wall Street and will only judge the process by the financial numbers.

You need to drive cost, quality, delivery and you need to make sure it shows up on the income statement and the balance sheet.

Isn't that hard to do, especially early in the process?

KOENIGSAECKER: When you start the process it takes a lot of energy and most of the organization will give you some level of support for improving quality and delivery. But in the end, productivity growth is the one that drives margin improvement and increases wealth, and you find out that nobody wants to do that. There are all kinds of dynamics you have to deal with. Those on the administrative side don't even think productivity is a relevant measure for them, and they don't want anything to do with it.

You have to push pretty hard on the results and at the same time you have to make sure that people are putting the infrastructure in and are using the tools. It can be uncomfortable, and most people will just pass on that discomfort unless there is some form of pressure. I use the results as pressure.

Is that what you did while leading the effort at the HON Company?

KOENIGSAECKER: At HON, we deployed an objective for every unit including administrative to improve output per person by 15 percent every year and to cut quality defects by 20 percent. When we got our lead time down to daily production it was harder to measure.

Most of the people thought we were insane when we started with those goals. Nobody liked them. To the extent that it doesn't spread is a management issue and that is where we as an industry need the most help.

Do you need hard-ass managers to make it happen?

KOENIGSAECKER: When you start in a new organization, one way or another, you have to make sure that everyone in the organization and especially the antibodies know that their choice is to join up with this new way or find a different organization. Most managers are very much afraid of making that decision.

You need to make sure it shows up on the income statement and the balance sheet.

To the extent that it doesn't spread is a management issue.

If you look at the history of mass production, it took about a generation after the idea started for it to be accepted.

Do you think it is inevitable that manufacturing will evolve to a lean system?

KOENIGSAECKER: If you look at the history of mass production, it took about a generation after the idea started for it to be accepted. After Ford, it was about a generation — 25 to 30 years — before GM and the others were on the same page and then it was another generation — post World War II — before the European auto manufacturers really adopted mass production. If you're in an industry and one firm in the industry adopts lean, they'll end up dominating the industry and other people will either have to do it or fall out of the industry.

If U.S. manufacturers start adopting lean, do you think it will lead to a revival of U.S. manufacturing?

KOENIGSAECKER: With lean, you end up with an extremely flexible and responsive company so that you can do things with delivery performance that were not possible at a long distance from your customers. That becomes a marketing advantage.

Using lean, you can get to daily production like they do at Danaher and HON where they make every product every day by going through reducing set up times, a la Shingo's methodology. At Jake Brake, for instance, Caterpillar or Cummins can call up a UAW operator in the cell and order product for the next day and it will be shipped the next evening.

When you start it seems impossible, but when you finish you realize it's pretty straightforward.

LEAN ENTERPRISE INSTITUTE INC.

The Machine That Changed The World: The Story of Lean Production, How Japan's Weapon in the Global Auto Wars Will Revolutionize Western Industry remains a seminal book that shook American manufacturing to its roots. In that work, published in 1990, the three directors of MIT's International Motor Vehicle Program coined the term "lean," and statistically revealed the benefits of Toyota's production system by comparing proprietary data provided to them by the world's major automobile manufacturers. The results were startling then and remain so today. Lean automobile production required less than half the human labor, half the manufacturing space, half the investment tools and half the engineering hours to produce a vehicle that was in many categories far better than anything produced using traditional mass production techniques.

James Womack, one of the authors of *The Machine That Changed The World*, is the country's leading proponent of lean manufacturing. He is now a principal of the Lean Enterprise Institute in Brookline, Mass. He is co-author with Daniel Jones, also of the Lean Enterprise Institute, of *Lean Thinking*, a book published by Simon and Schuster in 1999, of which more than 250,000 copies have been sold.

It's hard to fix total systems.

I created a little bit of a monster with the "Lean Thinking" book.

What are the major obstacles companies must avoid in trying to adopt a lean manufacturing system?

WOMACK: One thing you have to do as a manager is not lie to yourself about value. You must look at all of the things that you do and say how many of these actually create value and then eliminate those things that do not add value. Management is about getting closer and closer to perfection, which is exactly what the customer wants, with no waste.

It's hard to fix total systems. Why don't you do employee empowerment? That's a good fad. Why don't you do Six Sigma? To me they all tend to be focused on one piece of the system and what we try to do is to encourage people to look at the whole.

Do you see many successful lean implementations?

WOMACK: You get the application of lots of lean microtechniques that tend not to have very much effect. I go to companies and they tell me how many kaizens they've done and I say that's like telling me how long you've had your ISO certification. As a customer, so what? Is the product cheaper? Better? Can you get it for me quicker? Can you make me exactly the one I want? Those are the relevant questions to the customer, not how many kaizens you have done.

I feel I've created a little bit of a monster with the *Lean Thinking* book in the sense that we say very clearly that what you need to do is find a change agent. How about you? We say you need to get some knowledge because there really is some knowledge there that you need. We say you have to draw a map of the value stream of your product, and then we say: Now do something.

What most people left out was draw the map and look at the whole. They went straight to "do something." You end up with what we call Kamikaze kaizen, which is disconnected applications.

Do you have any examples of such Kamikaze kaizen?

WOMACK: I saw a great one the other day in a company that had done a set-up time reduction which was quite dramatic on a big machine that had one part number going through it. So you say, "Well, gosh, wow, what's that going to do for you?" Of course, nothing. The answer was, "It was technically challenging and we had extra time available. The machine hours were available so we could screw around with it."

I've seen many flip charts from companies highlighting their 70 percent reductions in inventory due to kaizen projects, but the company isn't performing any better.

WOMACK: By the way, is the 70 percent reduction sustainable? Does the customer ever notice that? What you typically have is that, "We were able to speed things up over here so they could sit longer down here." Yet nobody even seems to see it. That is a higher level of dysfunction.

I can't tell you how many people I've gone to see who want to tell me about their set-up time reduction. "We can change this machine over in three minutes." Of course you're standing there talking about something else and in the back of your head and in the corner of your eye you note that it seems to be taking them 20 minutes. You say, "You just told me three minutes." And they say, "Yeah, but there is a special condition right now."

Others tell me about how they cut inventory by 70 percent, but you see all of this stuff sitting there. "Well, we've had an anomalous situation today, but normally..." Well you know that is not true. Yet the funny thing is many people are not even lying to you. In their head they believe they do three-minute set ups and have a 70 percent inventory reduction.

I can't tell you how many cells I've been taken into and seen that what they've got are some adjacent machines that used to be in a strict process village layout. Now they are all close to each other and you pile up the inventory between each one. You say, "I don't think that is quite what [Taiichi] Ohno [inventor of the Toyota Production System] meant." They say, "Well, we're working on it." And I say, "Okay, you keep working on it."

Is lean having an overall impact on U.S. industry?

WOMACK: We put together a very interesting chart on inventory. It shows turns in the entire U.S. manufacturing economy. When you adjust for the business cycles, little has happened in the last 30 years.

What has happened quite strikingly is the car industry has done a very good job when you're looking at the materials on hand and work in process, which has gone from about 14 turns to about 24 over the space of about 10 years. That is quite significant and it's distinctly different from the pattern in general manufacturing.

The car guys started paying attention around the recession of 1981. The thought of oblivion focused their minds so that there now is a steady trend to do the right thing in the fabrication side of the car industry. If you look at 60-day finished units of vehicles out on the dealer lots nothing has happened there, although it eventually will.

People tell me about how they cut inventory by 70 percent, but you see all of this stuff sitting there.

Inventory turns have not changed much over 30 years.

Why have you not seen much of an impact in inventories given that there has been such a surge toward contract manufacturing, just-in-time and building-to-order?

WOMACK: Part of that is a variety effect in that the amount of stuff in every product category continues to increase. Inventories go up because you have to have inventory behind every different product. If you look at wholesale and retail in the United States, inventories have increased in the 80s and 90s in relation to sales because of variety.

Inventories go up because of the increase in product variety.

Are there any good examples of lean implementations other than Toyota in the U.S. automotive sector, given your own expertise in that area?

WOMACK: At going from bar stock to parts assembled on the car, really there has been a steady improvement and you see it quite consistently. We've been working with Delphi as a corporate partner and three years ago I would say there was hardly anything other than orthodox mass production at Delphi. But over the last three years — and this was not my doing — they hired some ex-Toyota guys to help them.

Parts of Delphi have done things I never thought they could have done. I could take you to Wichita Falls, Texas, and you would see a plant that runs on a pure pull system that has cellularized activities that were formally done in process villages the size of city blocks. They've taken their throughput time down by 90 percent. You couldn't have seen that anywhere in this country prior to 1990 and not really before the mid 90s.

How about the Michael Dell approach of building to order?

WOMACK: Dell is very lean from the assembly line to the customer and my understanding is he has done nothing from the assembly line back to raw materials. If you read Dell's book he always makes the suppliers locate close to him. If you go to Austin, look at the building called the "Revolver." It is one of the world's biggest warehouses on the backside of the assembly operation owned by a third-party logistics firm. There are acres and acres and acres of parts all sourced from East Asia where you get 20 days of just straight shipping time unless you are doing air freight.

Dell has done a terrific job of going from order-assembly to customer. He got that part right. The harder part is to go from the assembly operation back all the way to raw material. That is not a rap on Dell. Practically nobody in the world except Toyota in Toyota City has ever really done the thing whole hog.

Dell is very lean from the assembly line to the customer but not from the assembly line back to raw materials.

Will the whole thrust toward e-commerce lead to a much broader embrace of lean thinking?

WOMACK: Anybody can design a good Web site and do fulfillment off the Web. The nightmare is getting the stuff from in the ground to a finished product in your driveway. You see guys like Amazon spending literally billions building warehouses to do physical fulfillment. These are guys who never thought about fulfillment while they were designing the Web site and now they say, "We've got a lot of sales. How are we going to do this?" The answer is they don't know what to do.

Lean is the other half of the equation. You can't get away with no warehousing, but doing automated gargantuan facilities is the sure way of going bankrupt. That's what you're seeing these e-commerce guys doing.

Does the recent interest in supply chain management linked to the Internet fit well with lean thinking?

WOMACK: It's just amazing that so many people think that the problem was the fax machine wasn't good enough and that what you really need is everybody to be on the Web. That makes things better potentially, but not if you don't have some sort of order smoothing system and an instant response capability with your suppliers.

So much of the supplier management stuff is just another face on margin squeezing. You proclaim that we now know — and we didn't know before — how much waste there is in your operations and so therefore take it out and give us a big price down. That was what [former GM vice president of worldwide purchasing Ignacio] Lopez was doing with PICOS. He would come in and after three days and a cloud of dust discover that you had three extra people on the A-B-C process and then say, "We can take out 30 percent of the cost so just give us the money right now."

There is a long, long history of supply chain management that turns out to be nothing but a squeeze play. I'm always very skeptical talking about supply-chain management and partnership if you naively think you can do it with a little bit of Web linkage.

Many companies are solving their production problems either by contracting out manufacturing to companies like Solectron or shifting it to low-labor cost areas like Mexico. Is this a good way to fix a problem?

WOMACK: Most people don't have the ability to separate in their mind a true efficiency from doing it the same old crummy way with some people who haven't really heard about wages. For the long term, the only type of advantage that is sustainable is brilliant process management as opposed to rock bottom factor costs because those costs will change over time. Whereas if you keep it up and keep getting better, brilliant process management is with you no matter where you are. It's frustrating for a person like me to meet people who are otherwise very smart people who apparently just can't tell the difference.

The lean guy looks at the world and says something is really out of whack here. People have spent the 80s and the 90s doing labor content analysis and moved all things with any labor content to Sri Lanka. They end up with staggering logistics bills to haul this stuff back and forth and nobody knows how to total that up.

Go to final pack area in any plant and hold up a sample of the product and say, "Please tell me the total logistics cost of this product and show

E-Commerce does not reduce waste in the supply chain.

The only type of advantage that is sustainable is brilliant process management as opposed to rock bottom factor costs.

There is almost no direct labor content in any manufactured good.

me the total cost of managing all the handoffs that were required to take this thing all over the world and back." Nobody is even prepared to think about thinking about that. They have no way to think about it.

We routinely draw these maps going all the way back to raw material in which you have six months throughput time and 10,000 or 20,000 miles of travel and a kazillion handoffs between departments, plants, companies and regions. Is this really the best way to do things?

You say, "Why couldn't you just do all of these activities across the road?" And the answer is, "There is labor content in this product and we can't do anything across the road because labor costs too much."

You end up with this great enormous trade deficit, which is primarily entailed in containing labor cost.

Some smart people are eventually going to figure out that there is almost no direct labor content in any manufactured good at this point. What you have is a tremendous amount of logistics and managerial complexity costs. The talk about things like three-day cars and instantaneously built computers is mostly just pure hokum.

What you've got is an enormous pile of parts at the point of assembly which is quite demand responsive like Dell, and then if you just look at the back of the plant, they have three month's worth of stuff sitting there. They've got the world's most traditional supply chain that goes across the Pacific and they have a 747 that goes from Hong Kong to Austin every day. Is this the cheapest way to do things? I don't think so.

What are some common problems associated with implementing a lean system?

WOMACK: First off, most businesses were born as lean businesses because they had a single product designed by a couple of people in one room. As long as they had the single product and the single team they did great and sometimes you can extend that for a long period of time. The most notable example is Skunk Works where they had small, totally focused, ultra secret teams with desperate timetables and so therefore they were able to go very fast and consistently do brilliant things.

Companies are organized by process.

However, the interesting feature of life is that from your earliest success as a company, you're dragged in a different direction. Why don't we do multiple products and have lots of options and continuously deepen the technologies? That is all good. But then the natural way to do that is to basically organize by process; product engineering; manufacturing engineering; industrial engineering; sales; accounting; marketing; plating; stamping; and welding.

People are very comfortable with a process organization because it's a lovely conduit for career paths and portable skills. Pretty soon you know something that has economic value. Most human beings in their hearts feel most comfortable being in a skilled trade and that is as true of journalists, doctors and surgeons as it is of welders.

The last thing about skill trades is you have something down cold that is a method that you can perform yourself and make a living and, by the way, if you don't like your boss you can take it somewhere else.

That's not bad. It's just a fact. People feel very comfortable with process villages because it means you can talk to people who are like you. You can share experiences. There is a community. It means you have lots of villains — the upstream and downstream guys who if they would simply behave as you do everything would be fine.

So there is a psychology there that says teams are great so long as I don't have to seriously take my career to one. The team idea is a horizontal thing. Here's the problem: There is no career path for a multi-skilled team player. You have a job as long as you have a product and maybe the product fails or the company merges and now what are you going to say [to your next potential employer]? "I'm a good team player." Huh?

There is a great fear about skill dilution. I see it all the time. I see it with kaizen technicians who spend all of their time using negative advertising on each other. You never met a lean guy who ever had anything good to say about another lean guy's technique. The way you get business is you run down the other fellow. So even in the lean world, I see the desire to be a skilled tradesman.

For instance, here is a guy who is Mr. Setup Reduction, so everything is a setup problem. Here is Mr. Bottleneck Analyzer, so everything is a bottleneck problem. Everybody has a tool that they're going to go around and do whatever they can with that tool.

Americans talk about teamwork so much because we're so terrible at it. Our primary identification is with ourselves and our career.

The one little cultural bit that the Japanese had going for them which is deteriorating now was that their primary identification was with their company. It was easier for them to say, "Hey, go do something that isn't in your skill area because we're going to take care of you." Whereas, no one thinks that any company has the individual employee's interest very high on its list of priorities.

How do you overcome this problem?

WOMACK: We've been trying to create a new profession called the value-stream manager — the horizontal leader who says my job is to optimize the whole. We know most companies have tried experiments with matrix organizations where you are loyal to the product and loyal to your function and we know the function always wins because that is where your career path lies.

So we've been trying to create careers for value-stream managers. We've done some experiments with some of our partner firms. But it seems to me that what the world needs now is a true career path for those who think horizontally and not just for those who think vertically.

Why is value-stream mapping becoming a new lean trend?

WOMACK: There is the plant manager who has a million things

Here's the problem: There is no career path for a multi-skilled team player.

A new profession called the value-stream manager.

Value-stream managers are advocates of the product.

going through his plant; there is the area manager; the manager in charge of assembly or molding or paint or machining. Then you have the function heads. They're not going to be able to look at the whole meat of the product, which is essentially a flow horizontally whereas all those people are organized vertically.

Certainly the sensei or the black belt can just take care of this, but the truth is they're there for short-term technical intervention. They're not actually going to see this happen day to day. That is the great weakness of the system in terms of who is going to be the advocate of the product as opposed to being the advocate of the function, the area or the department. That is why we talk about value-stream managers.

What specifically is the role of a value-stream managers?

WOMACK: There is this notion that you can turn your company on its side. Well, you just can't do that because the plain fact is the way humans organize knowledge is by functional expertise.

What we need is to assign somebody the task of looking at the whole — the flow of value all the way through the product from raw material to customer and in some cases from concept to launch and then through the sustainment cycle as well. Is there anybody looking at the whole thing, saying wait a minute, how is it getting from here to here and why are we doing this? Who's going to do that on a continuing basis?

We don't have to create a whole new big heavy-duty bureaucracy to do this. One person if you give him some space and time can figure it out. And they might have other responsibilities as well.

Isn't that the job of a sensei?

WOMACK: Right now, you have a tendency toward free-floating expertise, muda slayers who are out there wandering around like Wild West gunslingers. They can be senseis or black belts. Their techniques are fine, but how do you sustain it? The area manager or the plant manager or the function head can't keep their mind on this and they keep losing their focus. When you lose your focus, you go back to trying to keep all the people in your area busy. Are all of your machines running or is your plant fully booked because that is the way most accounting systems work where you have standard cost systems.

Regressing is easy.

It's not surprising that those people when given half a chance will go back to what I call point optimization, which means by God every machine is running, every worker is working and every engineer is engineering. Unfortunately, the product is sitting in queues or is flowing backwards.

Yet no one even seems to notice. After you go through an operation and get to the end, hold up the product and say, "Who is responsible for thinking about how this product gets through the system?" And the answer is, "Well, you want to talk to the assembly chief or the head of fabrication or the chief engineer." The question doesn't compute. They say,

"That's not the way we think about this." We say, "That's right and you're wrong."

In every organization, there ought to be somebody who has done the very simple thing of drawing a value-stream map for every product family and who then says what are we going to do right away to make this better and who is going to be around to keep following up and keep following up and keep following up so that in fact you do make it better? And once you made it better, you immediately start thinking about how to make it better still.

If lean is so great why is Japan's economy so bad?

WOMACK: If you look at the charts in *The Machine That Changed The World* you'll see that the variations between Japan, North America and Europe are much less than the variation within the regions. If you look at the Japan chart there is always one [superior performer] and by the way friends we can't really tell you who it is but it begins with a "T" and ends with an "A."

I think it's absolutely salutary that there is not any nationalism left in this debate. You don't hear the culture nonsense any more. The one thing that did have some validity was if you were a company man and the company told you to play every position on the field, that was easier than if you were a position/function man.

That aside, I don't think any of the culture stuff had anything to be said for it. All of the beating each other around the head on nationalistic grounds is gone for a moment.

What you see in Japan is lots and lots of bad manufacturing and some good manufacturing and for a long time nobody could really make that distinction. Now people can, which is progress.

Is Toyota still the world's shining example of lean?

WOMACK: Toyota's attitude is we've been at this for 50 years and give us another 50 years and we might actually become pretty good. Toyota's share in every market segment has gone up very slowly but steadily and it's going up again. It's a hard thing in this day and age when people are convinced that everything works at Web speed, to say, "This business of trying to learn how to manage value and to steadily get closer to what the customer considers value while you steadily take the waste out, is a career worth or work." It is not five minutes and you have a miraculous cure. It's hard for people to hear that.

So Toyota just keeps on keeping on and bless their hearts because if they didn't I wouldn't have anything to talk about.

Is the ISO 9000 quality standard improving manufacturing processes?

WOMACK: The problem with all these doggone standards is they are strictly inputs. I used to make jokes about ISO and said it's what hap-

Japanese companies do not have a lock on lean.

Getting rid of waste is a career worth of work.

pened when Dr. Deming got lost in Brussels.

All you have to do is show that you have a procedure and that you follow it and the fact that you're still making crap doesn't make a difference. You cannot flunk ISO for making bad products. Isn't that amazing?

What started off as not a bad idea turns out to be just another cost of doing business. At most companies it perhaps raises by a bit their process consciousness but it doesn't lead to any improvement.

What you really want to measure are outputs. Are you getting a more durable, better product quicker at less cost? No customer ever went in and said, "Gee, how much ISO is in this product?"

What do you think of Six Sigma?

WOMACK: There is nothing wrong with Six Sigma, but who is going to manage the application of these techniques in a coherent way across an entire value stream for a product so that you get sustainable results? That is where we fall down. We're great at three-day wonders, but we're just very lousy at sustaining anything.

What do you think of GE's Six Sigma effort?

WOMACK: The real strength of the company has been that [former CEO Jack] Welch picks one or two things and they just do those one or two things. GE has taken process management very seriously but the test of that is what happens now that Welch has left.

There were two critical players at Toyota, one was family member Eiji Toyoda, the other was Taiichi Ohno. When they both left active management at the end of the 70s the company just marched from victory to victory because that company created a system. The real question is did Jack actually create a system or is what we're seeing the effect of the force of one extraordinary personality. All credit to the guy — it's not a negative rap on Welch. But it is a very interesting question as to whether there is a system there as opposed to one superlative almost magician type of guy who can get results just from willpower, and we don't know.

General Motors worked brilliantly so long as Sloan was there. But GM started to lose share pretty much at the time Sloan left and they have been floating down for the last 30 years. Here was a guy who clearly was a genius and he claimed to have left a system, but was the system only operable by the genius?

Whenever you go to Toyota, what you hear from them is that they want a system that produces brilliant results from mediocre managers. That is their claim to fame. If you can do that, it is your meal ticket.

In speaking with people in industry about the difficulties of lean systems they ask basic questions such as what do you do with the production engineer in a lean enterprise?

WOMACK: There are lots of traditional categories of professional skills that it turns out you either don't need or they need to be quite dra-

There is nothing wrong with ERP systems.

matically transformed. Here's one: what do you do with the guy who has become the world's big whiz-bang on ERP? When SAP comes out with its MRP module you can also be an expert on the higher architecture of MRP — I mean, you're set for life, right?

And then Womack comes along and says there is nothing wrong with ERP systems whether you are using SAP, PeopleSoft or whatever, but why are you installing components and modules that you will never, ever need? And you say wait a minute, you don't need my skill? No, not really.

Another question I've heard raised in the auto sector about lean is how can a company deal with the problems associated with producing replacement parts for the after market in a way other than traditional make-to-stock?

WOMACK: Basically, you have to learn how to make small amounts and you have to learn how to get pure signal back from the users.

The problem with after market is that it goes through so many layers and each layer typically has big lot sizes and big triggers that when you get back to the poor guy who's making the stuff on Monday, the world apparently needs one million and then on Tuesday after you made a million, they say they don't need any and then on Wednesday half the stuff comes back. There are just fantastic whip-crack effects like response problems that so far have not really been tackled.

Toyota is the only company I know that has really done a thorough job of thinking through how to take the volatility out of the after market. They're now talking about making deliveries to dealers a couple of times a day. It's always worked that way in Japan. You bring your car into the shop in the morning. They diagnose the car and the parts come in at 10:00 from the parts warehouse. So the dealers don't have any parts at all.

How to serve the aftermarket.

And then the guys making parts for the out-of-production vehicles are told every day here's what you need to make to replenish what we've sold today.

That is a totally different world from this make-to-stock, or really make-to-guess world in which your customer keeps telling you to do things and then they change their mind and say, "Why did you do that?"

The poor manufacturer is going crazy because your order flow is essentially pure noise. You have no clue as to what the end customer really wants and neither does your distributor. So you end up with mountains of stuff, much of it obsolete, and all kinds of stuff flowing backwards as well as forward because you ship too much and now it comes back.

Why have you been so critical of the aerospace industry?

WOMACK: The aerospace industry discovered it better do something in the 1990s. Two of our big partners have been United Technologies and Lockheed Martin and I've had some very intense personal experience with Boeing trying to get them to do the right thing. I can't say I've succeeded.

Aerospace is beginning to come around to lean.

Here is an industry that is low volume, ultra high variety that was born as a continuous flow industry in the sense that they had one product with no options. Six or seven years ago when I went around aerospace, they had no time for me at all. They would say, "Lean is for car guys. It's high volume. Forget it."

And I said, "Fellows, I think you could quadruple your velocity here just by doing a few simple things." They said beat it. We looked and looked and looked and the only thing I could find to study in 1992 was Pratt and Whitney and that's because they were absolutely facing oblivion and they had accidentally come across these ex-Toyota guys and were really going to try to do something.

I'm on the platform down at the Av Week Aviation Expo every year in Long Beach and I get up and yell at them. Five years ago I was a lunatic and nut cake and now they all ask very respectable questions about what they should do. They haven't done it, most of them, but I've transitioned from being the lunatic fringe type of force to being something that is no longer "why" but "how."

Are there other good examples outside of automobiles?

WOMACK: One of the most interesting things that has happened recently is Alcoa's touting of the Toyota Production System. That's a real breakthrough because Toyota would tell you in Japan that while they got high quality out of their supply base, they never really made any progress in steel, aluminum, glass or resin in getting these guys to make small amounts frequently. Alcoa is the first materials company in the world that said it is staking its future on making exactly what you want exactly when you want it. That is a historic breakthrough that says to me the ideas are spreading.

The electronics sector always considers itself so superior to other manufacturing sectors. Are they leaders in lean production given their cycle times?

WOMACK: The electronics guys and the PC world are a whole lot more mature than they realize. They've been living in a performance world where if your chip could do more MIPs than the other guy's chip then you were fine. That's going to change very quickly. They are suddenly going to discover that customers are going to be demanding that they get what they want, when they want it, cheap, and by the way it has to work.

Computer companies are going to have to change very quickly.

The Lean Enterprise Institute has put together a reading list for those wanting to learn about lean manufacturing. LEI included eight titles, but modestly left off two that should be included: *Lean Thinking* and *The Machine That Changed The World*, both co-authored by LEI principal

James Womack. The book titles listed below should give executives "a shortcut to a complete education on lean," says LEI. They are:

- *From the American System to Mass Production*, David Hounshell
- *Ford Methods and Ford Shops*, Horace Arnold and Fay Faurote
- *The Toyota Production System*, Taiichi Ohno
- *The Evolution of a Manufacturing System at Toyota*, Takahiro Fujimoto
- *A Study of the Toyota Production System*, Yashuhiro Monden
- *The Toyota Production System*, Shigeo Shingo
- *Japanese Manufacturing Techniques*, Richard Shonberger
- *The New Manufacturing Challenge*, Kiyoshi Suzaki
- *The Machine That Changed The World*, James Womack, Daniel Jones and Daniel Roos
- *Lean Thinking*, James Womack and Daniel Jones

ALCOA INC.

Alcoa is perhaps the world's most revered metals company, and most of its success, say analysts, is due to its implementation of a lean business strategy. In the late 1990s, the company created the Alcoa Business System (ABS) and the Alcoa Production System, both of which were based upon the Toyota Production System.

ABS provides the company's 120,000 employees "with a structured system of working designed to eliminate waste, reduce inventories, cut costs, accelerate response time and deliver valuable competitive advantage to Alcoa's customers," says the company. Between 1998 and 2003, the system will save Alcoa $2 billion and has reoriented production to a "pull" model of responding to customer demand instead of building to inventory, an especially difficult approach for a metals company like Alcoa to implement. The company calls its system "produce for use, not for inventory."

Alcoa is seeing huge results in virtually every measurable category as a result of its newly installed system. Quality, cycle times, productivity, on-time delivery, scrap, worker injuries, inventory, customer complaints, delivery, environmental waste and capacity have all improved dramatically since the system was introduced in 1998. The ABS "is not a people-reduction initiative," says company CEO Alain Belda.

With sales in 2001 of $22.9 billion, Alcoa is managing to stay profitable despite a 13 percent decrease in aluminum prices, a 4 percent reduction in global output and increased competition from companies in low-cost areas of the world.

Keith Turnbull is the executive who introduced the new production and business system at Alcoa. But Turnbull doesn't like to use the word "lean," instead professing to be a student of the Toyota Production System. Turnbull, who has served in numerous technology positions at Alcoa including vice president of technology planning and executive vice president of strategic analysis and planning, is executive vice president of the Alcoa Business System and is in charge of implementing ABS throughout the company.

The Alcoa Business System has similarities to lean, but it is not lean.

The financial community recognizes that Alcoa has changed its business by practicing lean production techniques of building to order rather than building to inventory. Have your competitors taken notice?

TURNBULL: What we have done is to share with the analysts that we are using an improvement called the Alcoa Business System. We've shown them what we did and they thought that was neat and so they write about us and are talking about the changes we're making through the Alcoa Business System.

How have you gone about adopting lean?

TURNBULL: The Alcoa Business System has similarities to lean, but it is not lean. In most people's minds lean and the Toyota Production System are the same thing, but not in mine.

Why?

TURNBULL: They're very similar except that lean includes good ideas from here and there. Let's say I'm trying to implement the Toyota Production System and you come along with a good idea and it's in the general category of the TPS then that would be introduced and judged valid with respect to the word lean, but it may actually destroy some part of the system that we haven't yet learned. So when I get wiser, I'll be more open to other ideas.

How have you gone about your drive to adopt this new business system?

TURNBULL: We hired guys who knew the Toyota Production System to come in and help. We also have Toyota's help. It would take about 100 years on your own. I don't think we would have had the perseverance to keep making all the mistakes you make.

Given the size of your production processes, how difficult was it for your company to adopt a new production system?

TURNBULL: It's hard. You have to want to do it and then you have to have a lot of perseverance and knowledge. Then do it. It's not easy and almost nobody practices the Toyota Production System. Lots of people stop short of it.

Why?

TURNBULL: They don't understand it. There are huge misunderstandings as to what it is. You get part way into it and get into trouble and you don't understand the rest of the system and so before long you turn around and go back. Or you stay halfway there, stuck.

Has that been a problem with Alcoa's implementation?

TURNBULL: No. We keep learning more and more and we have a lot of help from Toyota.

Is the Alcoa Production System grounded in the broader ideas of lean manufacturing?

TURNBULL: I never use the term lean. My struggle with lean is that it includes a lot of nice ideas and I'm not smart enough to sort a lot of nice ideas back into a system. Toyota has a system and we try to use their system. I find it less confusing to use their system.

If I see three good ideas about lean and put them in, I might actually break the system without even knowing I did it while I'm still growing up and learning about it. So I won't take that chance. I don't do lean. I only do TPS. It's not because I'm arrogant, but because I'm not smart enough to convert a system for cars into aluminum and change it at the same time. It's too hard.

So how do you deal with basic lean principles such as takt time and 5-S?

TURNBULL: Those are requisite elements of the system, so of course we pay enormous attention to those.

How different is your operation today than it was when you first started implementing the Toyota Production System?

TURNBULL: We have factories that are profoundly different. They had a lot of inventory and long lead times and they had delivery perform-

You have to want to do it.

Toyota has a system and we try to use their system.

ance problems. We've converted them to produce any product any day. That is very different.

It's easy to say, but it's terribly difficult to do. There are instances where you can draw the drawing and see the design and then you can't have it for two years — there is something about the way the land is set, so you can't have it even though you can describe it. Other times you can have it as fast as you can draw it.

We have plants of both types. But more often the problem requires a belief in the system in order to do it. You have to believe in the system before you know the system because it's an integrated system, and you don't understand how all the wires connect. So our more rapid progress is made in those instances where we choose to trust the system as a capacity to change this business behavior and then we do it.

Is that change required of everyone within Alcoa?
TURNBULL: Only a few people have to buy in and a few people have to change. Some buy in and lead. There are others who don't really buy in but go along and that's okay. But you can't have the leaders say I won't go along, because it won't work. They have to buy in.

Is that the most difficult aspect of adopting the Toyota Production System?
TURNBULL: We have a chairman who buys in and changed our leadership around so that others that had bought in moved to new jobs. As they moved to new jobs they were directed to implement ABS as part of their arrival. They were trained ahead of time so they could arrive knowledgeable and go do it.

You were the one who provided the inspiration for the change, were you not?
TURNBULL: I'm the one who knew about it first. Alain Belda, who is now our chairman, was our president and COO and he decided that we weren't going to make the kind of business progress we needed without a system. Most people go out and buy a method and not a system, and he concluded that we needed a system. He concluded that the TPS was the most efficient in the world, so let's do that one. He decided to personally learn the Toyota Production System so that he could provide the leadership for it. He spent four months learning it.

Do you know of any other CEOs who have done that?
TURNBULL: A lot of them think they have but I don't know of many that have actually trained with such rigor.

With the Toyota Production System, is there a difficult transition to make between automobiles and aluminum?
TURNBULL: Some of it is real easy and other parts are real hard

To produce any product any day is easy to say, but it's terribly difficult to do.

Most people go out and buy a method and not a system.

depending on what part of the flow path you're in. When our flow path looks like discrete parts, all you have to do is change the name. When our flow path looks like pipes, it's harder but doable.

Where are you in the process?
TURNBULL: Just started. We removed $1.1 billion of our costs through ABS by the end of 2000. That is a big deal.

Does it cost much to do this?
TURNBULL: You don't need any new equipment or machinery. Everything remains the same.

How hard is it to use the same machinery and convert it to production on a "pull" basis?
TURNBULL: That is what most people learn first, but that is not the essence of the Toyota Production System. The first thing you typically address is flow and inventory. That's okay and that's fine, but the system is a lot deeper than that.

Are you pushing the concept into your supply base?
TURNBULL: Some.

Is it easy to do, or do they come in and learn the system?
TURNBULL: Toyota does that, but we're not into it that far yet.

How specifically do you learn the Toyota Production System?
TURNBULL: Directly straight from Toyota. They took me over to Japan and showed me what it was. We went to Brazil together and visited several factories together with Toyota as my trainer.

Do you pay them for this type of training?
TURNBULL: No. It's a symbiotic relationship.

From your perspective, are there companies that have done this well in the United States?
TURNBULL: Fewer than you think. There are a lot of leans, but not many TPSs. There is merit in getting a little lean and making progress. The only companies in the United States that have gotten close are suppliers to Toyota because Toyota has its Toyota Supply Support Center that converts suppliers to TPS. They work with 50 companies so those folks get taught by Toyota as part of Toyota's supply chain.

Are you part of that supply chain?
TURNBULL: We supply relatively little metal to them and we represent a big company, so we would be a lot of work for them. We don't have the relationship of them coming into our factory and sending their key

You don't need any new equipment or machinery.

There are a lot of leans, but not many TPSs.

people in as direct conversion people. They do treat us openly but without the commitment of their hours. That is how we are able to learn.

Is this how you would recommend others to learn about lean?
TURNBULL: It depends on if you want to learn about lean or the Toyota Production System. If you want to learn about lean, there are a lot of places to go. If you want to learn about TPS, then Toyota owns TPS and they share it with others.

How have you managed to save $1.1 billion using TPS?
TURNBULL: You save one dollar then you get two, then three then four.

How have you categorized the savings?
TURNBULL: You don't have to be pure; you can give or take $100 million and it's still worth your effort. We have not worried about precision of the measurement but about the size of the capture.

Do you measure inventory turns?
TURNBULL: We are deeper into inventory than we have been in a long time. We have gone down so low in inventory that we have been peeling away layers that haven't been touched for a long, long time.

How long is a long, long time?
TURNBULL: A decade.

What are your inventory turns?
TURNBULL: I don't know because we are divided into a bunch of business units that have their own turns. Aggregate turns are interesting, but the turns by business unit are the ones I pay attention to.

And those are improving?
TURNBULL: Yes, but the reason I linger is that it is a cheap approach to say you are lean and have driven inventory down. The question is: Did you help or hurt your system? If you haven't actually constructed a system, you may have a new inventory turn system and done a lot of damage.
The alternative is to go and understand the system. You have to put the system in place and let the system take the turns. In rare instances, inventory will go up if you put the system in, but it might need to. You'd rather have the system because it always goes down eventually.

How long before you get the Toyota Production System installed at Alcoa?
TURNBULL: One hundred years.

You don't have to be pure.

In rare instances, inventory will go up if you put the system in, but it might need to.

Toyota stays humble, and hungry.

Does Toyota have it installed system wide?

TURNBULL: I just spent a week with Toyota's key guys and we got to the last day and I asked them this same question. Here I am sitting across from the experts and they say the progress they made this year is so great that it demonstrates that we're mere learners. It is the humility. The design of the TPS is designed for the absolute elimination of waste, so against that target, that goal, the gap remains huge. So they stay humble and hungry.

WARNER ROBINS AIR FORCE BASE

The federal government is not known to be a hotbed for lean principles and applications. But lean does exist within one corner of the federal enterprise. The Warner Robins Air Force Base in Georgia has had early success with a lean implementation. Its experience points to what could become hefty savings for the federal government if lean is implemented throughout the military's hundreds of industrial sites. The commander of the facility, which has more than 19,800 employees and is the largest industrial complex in the state of Georgia, fully supports the lean way of thinking.

Maj. General Dennis Haines, described by some lean practitioners as being the leading lean luminary in the federal government, knows the lean lingo, from flow, to cellular manufacturing to takt time. He holds a lean breakfast with the leadership of each of his base's directorates every Friday morning at 6:30 a.m. He has participated in kaizen events on the factory floor, daily recap sessions and Friday report-outs. He has gotten to know firsthand the problems and constraints faced by workers and supervisors wrestling with the burden of government paperwork and bureaucracy.

Lean has an inherent aversion for rules and regulations and Haines has found that many such restrictions are unnecessary to improving the value streams of the hundreds of products moving through the four-million-square feet of maintenance shops at Warner Robins. The facility, on 8,722 acres in central Georgia, is tasked with keeping Air Force planes flying, including worldwide logistics support for the F-15, C-5, C-130, the U-2, all Air Force helicopters and missiles. Warner Robins also refurbishes all types of avionics and aircraft systems.

Due to budgetary constraints and the unwillingness of Congress to fund new aircraft initiatives, a great deal of pressure has been placed on Warner Robins to keep aircraft flying long beyond their conceived lifespan. Each plane that comes in to be refurbished presents a Pandora's Box of problems and the Air Force can't turn to vendors who no longer exist to produce replacement equipment. Organic engineering, reverse engineering and manufacturing of parts is a big and expensive part of the base's operations. Lean has the potential to reduce a lot of the headaches involved in addressing these difficult issues.

Lean operations have been introduced initially in the F-15 wing shop and the savings last year alone were a reported $8 million. The concept is now being fanned out to other areas, including avionics.

Beyond Warner Robins, the Air Force Materiel Command is studying lean as a business system, as are other Air Force logistics centers, with the encouragement and funding dollars from the Air Force Manufacturing Technology Directorate at the Air Force Research Laboratory in Ohio.

The Air Force was wondering whether we could do our business.

Is there a future for lean in the military's industrial complex?
HAINES: I think so. I like the lean thought process. I like the way it forces you to examine what you're doing to identify what you're really about, the end product you're producing and the essential steps to produce it.

What propelled Warner Robins into considering adopting a lean approach to its operations?
HAINES: For us, our first thrust has been in manufacturing and repair because that is where we had the biggest need for a catharsis. We had far too much of what we were producing coming out late and with costs increasing. Increasingly, our customer — the Air Force — was looking at us wondering whether we really knew what kind of business we were in and whether we could do that business. Even though we felt we

I have seen the power of lean.

Savings are in the millions.

were competitive with the other people in the business, it was pretty much apparent to us that we needed to change.

How long have you personally been involved in the lean way of thinking?

HAINES: I've become familiar with lean only in the last couple of years and have seen the power of it. We had lean prototype programs going here for the past year and a half at the wing shop and one in the avionics area. The wing shop was getting good management support. But in terms of senior-level involvement, there was literally none for the first six months — we simply weren't aware of what was going on.

Is that knowledge beginning to percolate into the management ranks at Warner Robins?

HAINES: Absolutely, dramatically. We are fortunate in that we have some good benchmarks within the organization now so we can show people the befores and the afters and the dramatic changes as a result of implementing lean.

What are some of your success stories?

HAINES: The F-15 wing constitutes almost half of the man-hours and the cost of an F-15 depot maintenance program because it has to be literally completely rebuilt. The scheduled time to do that in order to meet the airplane flow is 37 days. A year and a half ago when we started with lean, we were on a seven-day-a-week, three-shift operation and still could not meet the production-line requirement.

So the Air Force's F-15 system program manager who runs the whole worldwide support system was looking for a second source for F-15 wings with the idea of starting them up and if they did better work than us, they would move a lot of it to that organic facility.

Today, we're doing the same number of wings in the 37 days, but we're doing it in a five-day, two-shift operation — 16 hours a day. We've moved 25 people out of that production area to other areas where we needed them. We reduced our overtime expense by $1.5 million; we saved another $1.5 million by the people we moved out of the area; and surprisingly enough when we went to the cellular, one-piece flow, we went from individual toolkits and multiple pieces of special equipment, to equipment specialized for that particular portion of the flow and we saved $1.2 million in tools.

The potential applications must be vast at Warner Robins, given the 14 million square feet of industrial space there.

HAINES: My view is that in every area that we measure in production we will have the same kind of results. In the first cut, we will average 30 percent reduction in costs and a 30 percent reduction in flow days, and it's proven true with every one we've done so far.

How hard will that be to achieve base-wide? How long will it take?

HAINES: It will take some time to get through the entire process because it's very focused, very intensive. We have a weekly senior-level meeting on lean just to keep our focus on it and to talk about how fast we can move through it.

We started with essentially one team in each major production area and are building on that core. We have a lean event and then through the successes like we had in the wing shop, where people have gone through the process and have learned how to do that process, we use a portion of that savings as our seed corn. From those 25 people who worked it through the wing shop, we picked three to run new teams.

In the product directorate where the F-15 wing work is done, which we call Technology and Industrial Support, I have seven teams running in a production unit of 2,500 people. But there are 150 separate shops, each of which has multiple processes. It will take a couple of years to do it the first time in each of those shops and do it right. And then you're ready to go through it again.

Where else have you expanded the effort?

HAINES: One other team has just finished in C-5 floorboards area. We did a lean event and we increased the throughput by 40 percent and decreased material costs by 30 percent.

Are there any intangible benefits to the lean approach to your operations?

HAINES: We had lost a lot of the real in-depth communication between the employees and the supervisors. Lean forces the supervisors, the workforce and the support people on a team to all start working things as a team and thinking of themselves as a team. Our people who work the process know what to do and they know where the good ideas are, we just have to tap that. One of the real secrets of lean is it opens that communication.

The second is the ability to go into a process with a clean-sheet approach with no constraints. I'm going to build a process that works and then we'll worry about changing the rules, regulations and policy to support a process that works. When you do that, all kinds of internal constraints that you've built in for what at the time seemed to be good reasons become counter productive. When you look at this as a one-piece flow — as a value stream — these constraints become counter productive.

You start identifying all of those internal hurdles that senior management can simply change. People think that they are rules constrained, but when we look at it, about 80 percent of all those constraints we can do away with ourselves. There are about 20 percent that we have to go to somebody else and educate and try to change, but the vast majority we find we can fix.

We have a weekly senior-level meeting on lean just to keep our focus on it.

Lean forces supervisors and workers to start working as a team.

How many of the rule changes require an act of Congress?

HAINES: There are very few that are law. There are a few more that are OSD policy or Air Force policy, but most of them are our policy and our procedures. That is enlightening to a lot of folks when we go through the first time because they think, "Well, we can't change those," and we find that we can.

The third piece is that when you make changes happen quickly, it gets the workforce's attention, and they know that the management is supportive, interested and involved. When you do those three things, magic happens.

It must make coming to work more interesting and fun.

HAINES: I just came out of one of our meetings and that is exactly the sentiment that is coming out of my production chiefs. They are now going down there and even if it's not a lean event, they're walking value streams themselves, saying this process isn't working, so let me just walk each of the steps through. It's kind of like the flat forehead where you keep hitting yourself in the forehead: Why am I doing that? Why am I doing that?

Can an organization like yours initiate a lean implementation on its own or do you need help doing it?

HAINES: You need help doing it and we have one of the best, we're using Simpler Consultants. This was one of our learning experiences, too. One of our hiccups early on was we didn't have the strongest consultants on our effort and so as we became smarter and more insistent, we put a first team on it. Our objective is to let them teach us for a year or so and by then we should have our own people who are ready to start running with it internally.

How did you personally come to your enlightened state?

HAINES: I was exposed a little bit to it when I was the Air Force Materiel Command director of logistics. At the time, the book *The Machine That Changed the World* came out and I read it. I was embroiled in things that we thought would improve our efficiency. At the time we were working on the Depot Repair Enhancement Program and Contract Repair Enhancement. Both focused on improving the production and the support to production and supply chain management. So I've been working that issue for a long time, but I didn't really get excited about implementing lean itself until I got here and I became aware of the project we were doing.

George Koenigsaecker [former CEO of The HON Co.] came down here for a two-day seminar and this was the catharsis. Here is one of the leading guys in lean in the United States and he came down here and shared two days with us and because of the low level that lean was being worked here, I really didn't know what was going on. I found out about it

When you make changes happen quickly, it gets the workforce's attention.

Haines's "catharsis."

I was on fire after reading "Lean Thinking."

You can always have setbacks. Old habits die hard.

at the last minute. Our senior staff didn't really know that his seminar was designed for us. We just had the wrong people working it.

I sat through a portion of that because I had conflicts and I hadn't even cleared my schedule for two days. So we missed an opportunity. I asked George to come back and we had another two-day session. Prior to that two-day session, we all read *Lean Thinking* by Womack and we sat down for two days with George, and I was on fire. I was on fire after reading the book and saying yes, this is the way I approach my thinking. I think it will work for us, let's go try.

Was it easy to see the connections between a Wiremold type of industrial case study and your processes?

HAINES: We think of ourselves as having this unique problem in the repair business in that nothing is repeatable, but when you look at what we do it's very repeatable. There are some surprises, but a lot of the surprises come by our not examining what we were doing and not planning well enough. Lean has forced us to do that. We're starting to tackle some of the really tough areas now and so I'm excited. It will fundamentally change our performance.

Is lean becoming institutionalized at Warner Robins?

HAINES: Quickly. It is not institutionalized at every level in every activity, but I have enough of the senior management staff who are truly getting excited about this so I think it will last when I'm gone.

How about the traditional cultural change that is required?

HAINES: There is a long way to go, a long way to go. Those areas that are in it and are using it, they're believers. But I'll tell you though, you can always have setbacks, even in the areas that are the most mature. We just went through a period in our wing shop where the F-15s were pushing up their production so we had to shorten our flow days and instead of really sitting back and figuring out that we've got to change our takt time, what does that mean for each piece, we fell back to throwing overtime and throwing people at it. They got out of sync and guess what? Our efficiency of operation went way down. So we said, oops, we did that wrong, let's get back to basics.

We went back to the one-piece flow and now we're back on track. So even in the mature shops you have to watch the fact that the old habits die hard.

How are you training your people?

HAINES: We're now massively deploying it with massive training. What we're trying to avoid is building a lot of up-front costs, so a lot of our training in this is just in time: you train and then you go into an event. The training is recent and you reinforce it by experience. I've been involved too many times where we go in and give everybody four days of training and then they didn't use it for a year and it is forgotten and we just wasted it.

How has lean changed your own individual job?
HAINES: Let me say I have not made as much of a catharsis as I know I need to make and I would like because I'm fighting schedule every day. But what I am finding is that I'm taking my schedule almost once a week and building white space into it where I can go down and visit a lean activity, participate at least a little bit in a lean shop.

[I] have my secretary say he's not here and [I] actually do [a] full-up lean event. We're making the same commitment among all of our senior leadership here, where we will do at least one lean event ourselves a quarter. They will participate in their lines plus one a quarter outside.

The area that we have missed so far is getting the second-line supervisors involved in a lean event. Thus far, they've been taking the lean briefings, they'll take the end-of-day briefing and the final lean team briefing, but there is a difference between being informed and having ownership. So we're getting them involved more in actually doing the lean events. Organizationally, we're at the beginning of a transformation into being a really lean oriented organization.

How shocking is it for the people working the line to see you down there with them?
HAINES: They are getting used to seeing a general on the line since I've been here. When I got here nearly two years ago and walked down on the line the first time, especially when I walked in without an entourage of people with me, it was a shock to them. But they're used to it now.

That's what leadership is all about.
HAINES: Every time I go on the line I learn something and I find that something is not exactly like I had expected. Sometimes it's really heartening because it's something really good going on. More often than not it's an area where I can help resolve a constraint when something is going not as I thought it was going.

When you're doing your week-long lean event, are you outfitted like a major general or dressed like someone who is working the line?
HAINES: When I participate in a lean event, they know who I am so I might as well wear the uniform, but I am quite aware of the fact that I can easily dominate a forum like that just because of the position; so at least my initial view is that I'll be more in the role of a facilitator and encourager in that process and let them do the talking.

Does it make it more difficult to have success when someone of your stature is down on the floor with the line workers? Do they hesitate

We're at the beginning of a transformation.

Every time I go on the line I learn something.

and wonder about what they should say and what it is they're doing?

HAINES: There is initially some discomfort but that goes away within the first couple of hours. They forget you're wearing the rank in terms of their being open and feeling at ease at making comments. The more senior you get, the more important it becomes how you go into the group and how you present yourself. If you go in and do a lot of talking and dominate it, you'll probably inhibit the process.

Do the workers try to hide their blemishes, thinking, "Oh boy, this process isn't very good and we've worked it for 20 years so we better try to make it look better than what it is."

HAINES: I don't think so.

Does the old command-and-control military mentality make it hard for you to get management to work together with workers?

HAINES: I don't know that lean attacks that particularly. One of the things that we find that is an inhibitor in the process is trust. To really get lean, you have take some of those constraints off and trust the person doing it to have made the right decision.

There is another part of lean that helps you do that. If you build lean right, in terms of one-piece flow, the constraints and the problems are going to be elevated so quickly to you that it doesn't have time to really get out of bounds and out of control before it's up to senior management. That is a good thing because right now in a normal process, you can be so far behind you can't recover before a senior manager finds out.

What can other managers in government industrial operations learn from your experience?

HAINES: You just have to dig in and do it yourself. You have to go see other people who are doing it and the light bulbs will come on.

It's interesting how we're talking about a mode of operation that is called "lean." The benefits are real, but the term "lean" doesn't seem to fit the process. Toyota doesn't even call it lean. They call it the Toyota Production System.

HAINES: From the Air Force standpoint it's unfortunate that it carries that moniker. I've been looking for another name because we started with lean logistics in 1995 and we leaned everything before we fixed the processes. We really hurt our readiness.

So when people talk lean, the paradigm of that goes back to those old things and this lean is not that lean. This lean is really fix the process, resource the value-added process and eliminate the non-value-added processes.

People think it's just another way to cut costs or lay off workers, but it's much bigger than that. If someone could come up with a descriptive name other than lean it would be helpful.

To really get lean, you have to have trust.

This lean is not that lean...

DELPHI CORP.

Delphi Corp., the world's largest producer of auto parts and components, has experimented with many different manufacturing systems over the years, including the Theory of Constraints, TQM, agile manufacturing and others. But it has settled on lean.

Spun off from GM as an independent company in 1999 and with sales in 2001 of $26.1 billion, Delphi has been working closely with the Lean Enterprise Institute to perfect a system based upon value-stream mapping of its processes. The person in charge, Dave Logozzo, director of manufacturing operations, says the technique has led to a rebirth of manufacturing as a profession.

Plant managers have to let us know what they're going to do over the next 12 weeks.

Value-stream maps are a much better tool to identify waste than any we've ever seen.

How is Delphi applying lean?

LOGOZZO: At the manufacturing level at our 180 sites around the world, we have made value-stream mapping and one-page site plans for current and future states mandatory for all of our businesses on a quarterly basis.

The plants that are more mature in the process are drawing maps at the department level. We require one from a corporate viewpoint to be sure everyone is learning and understanding quarterly. Plant managers have to sign off quarterly to let us know what they're going to do over the next 12 weeks. The normal auto industry mentality was the five-year plan, now it's the 12-week plan.

How do you use the value-stream maps?

LOGOZZO: We use them as the guide. Even when J.T. Battenberg takes a tour as the CEO we show him the value-stream map of the current state and the future state and how we're working to get to the future state.

Within each of the divisions we've named at the highest executive level business-line executives who are the value-stream owners. These are people without staffs. We're organized by functions: manufacturing, engineering, finance. But the P&L responsibility now lays in the hands of this business-line executive. The concept is they take their value stream and by their influence and by what is needed in the value stream they go figure out where to put all the resources of the functions.

What have you learned from these value-stream maps?

LOGOZZO: We've learned that they are a much, much better tool to identify waste than any we've ever seen. The value-stream maps are an eye opener on waste. The second thing is the material and information flow is the priority. Information and material flow is king. As we do the value-stream maps, we concentrate on the material and information flow.

How do you map these flows?

LOGOZZO: It requires an understanding of the concept and then going out on the floor and asking questions. When you get into the overriding IT system, for instance MRP, then it's complex and takes a different skill set. But to draw the map on the basic information flow is fundamental.

How hard was it to settle on a lean operating strategy having practiced other concepts like Theory of Constraints, and agile manufacturing?

LOGOZZO: Both our chairman J.T. and [president] Don Runkle have said at our annual leadership conference that lean is plan A, and plan A, and there is no backup plan or plan B. There is a strong message there. In manufacturing engineering that's what we're banking on.

Is value-stream mapping the silver bullet of lean?

LOGOZZO: I keep telling our people that you have to be humble and once you consider yourself a lean expert, then consider yourself not to be one. There is no end. The map points out what to do in current state versus future state. Once you get to the future state, you draw another map and the better you get at it, the more future state you'll have. This is not a one-shot deal. There is no end to it.

What we've found is how useful the tool is as an ongoing tool — a philosophy of how you look at improvement versus it being an engineering thing that you draw up a couple of times per year.

What have you discovered through your value-stream mapping exercises?

LOGOZZO: We have found an awful lot of capacity that basically we didn't know we had before. We found a lot of ways to get improvement and material information flow without having to make capital investments. That is a bigger bang for the buck than trying to measure reductions in inventory. We have also learned that it is valuable in product development.

How do value-stream maps of a manufacturing process help in product development?

LOGOZZO: This is my biased opinion, but over the last 20 years our product engineers have lost the ability to design a part that can be built cost effectively. We have lost the ability to take the variation out and have good quality. Now we have our product and manufacturing engineers drawing the maps, and they have become much, much more business oriented. They are now coming back saying, "You're asking me to be an engineer again." Instead of just designing the product, they are getting back into the nitty gritty, talking to people on the floor and asking how they make this stuff flow.

I've found this to be one of the better tools to get product designers working with manufacturing. It puts things in a great context because it includes the customers' perspective. If you don't have the customers' expectations and takt time, then your map is not going to be very good.

As markets turn down will you be able to respond more easily to changes in demand?

This is not a one-shot deal.

Product and manufacturing engineers have become much more business oriented.

LOGOZZO: That's the ideal state. We're not there by any stretch of the imagination but we understand it better.

Delphi has 180 plants around the world and we have wide variation, but the basic process of the value-stream mapping and the quarterly reviews we do is universal and the international people pick up on the concept very quickly. I managed many of our international operations for quite a few years and they are more used to drawing diagrams and communicating in that manner. When you bring in a tool like the one John Shook and Mike Rother developed [*Learning to See* from the Lean Enterprise Institute], they're off and running.

Do you see this as becoming part of the American manufacturing culture within Delphi?

LOGOZZO: I see this as a rebirth of manufacturing as a profession in the United States because it's a manufacturing tool that takes more of a business perspective and makes you link up to the customer. All the other tools that we use such as Six Sigma and Theory of Constraints, which still has its place, are excellent tools. But when you draw the value-stream map, it makes you connect everything. Someone is out there with the greatest tools, and we're fortunate that we have them, but if they're not connected to your overall material and information flow, you have to say, please explain to me why I'm doing that.

How do you confront the make-versus-buy question in a lean enterprise?

LOGOZZO: We have the business line executives who are doing the value-steam mapping try to identify competencies because everyone will be doing some insourcing and outsourcing. What are the processes you keep in house and which ones do you outsource? We're asking them to take a business perspective and then let the chips fall where they may on cost elements and so forth.

Do these value-stream managers feel like a fish out of water?

LOGOZZO: They are new but they will tell you that they prefer running the business this way and they wouldn't go back to a structure without it once they understand the value of it.

Do they carry weight in order to make decisions and execute the maps?

LOGOZZO: Typically they are on the executive staff reporting to the presidents of our six divisions. They're at as high a level in the organization as anyone in the operating units. Their peer group would be the CFO or the engineering director in the division.

Are there any software tools to help draw up the value-stream maps?

I see this as a rebirth of manufacturing as a profession in the United States.

I want the *floor people* to understand their scheduling and do it themselves.

LOGOZZO: It's very sporadic. We're looking for the software systems — the middleware — to the SAP blocks outside the plant. Internal to the plant, we're doing our own. Quite frankly, I really don't want to link the backend ERP with the plant floor stuff. I want the floor people to understand their scheduling and do it themselves.

Barry Controls of Brighton, Mass., a $74-million producer of equipment that controls shock, vibration and noise, started its lean manufacturing journey in 1998, and it has not been easy. But a difficult transition period is beginning to bear fruit for the 300-employee manufacturer of systems sold to aerospace, defense and industrial markets. The company has spent millions of dollars on new presses, an Oracle business software suite and lean systems training for its employees, but it's biggest challenge is overcoming an ingrained manufacturing system.

Company president Dan Yurovich joined Barry Controls in 1998 as vice president of operations, having served as a plant manager at NewellRubbermaid. When the 58-year-old company was purchased in 1999 by Hutchinson Manufacturing, a division of TotalFinaElf Group of France, Yurovich, who spent 15 years in the Marines, was promoted to the top position of the company.

It's been a journey.

Two old salts who have been here 18 years and 25 years are making the changes now.

Is your lean implementation on track?
YUROVICH: It's primarily been an operational function and has not been embraced by the rest of the company. Now that I have been promoted to president and GM of the company, the culture change will happen a little more effectively than in the past. We have hired a person who we specifically call our kaizen champion and coordinator. We started attacking through 5-S and kaizens making things visual, reducing waste, cleaning out the entire plant facility. It's been a journey.

How far along are you from your goal of being a lean enterprise?
YUROVICH: We're probably 15 to 20 percent along the timeline from order entry through to shipping. If I get to 50 or 60 percent in two to three years I will be ecstatic.

How hard was it to implement the lean techniques within the operations of a mid-sized company?
YUROVICH: Up front, it was not fun. It was ugly. We had a lot of demographic issues going on. We had just put in a new computer system that brought us to our knees. When we went live with our new computer system about 15 months ago, we went blind. We became almost a month-and-a-half late on shipments to customers and we worked through that at the same time we tried to change a culture.

That aside, it's been exciting when you look at two old salts on the shop floor who have been here for 18 years and 25 years respectively. They're making the changes now. These old supervisors who would just as soon bite your head off are now working through the process.

How hard is it to transform a traditional manufacturing culture?
YUROVICH: You have to persevere, believe in what you're doing and have a supportive boss. It would be better if the philosophy came from the corner office. He has to support it even though he might not be out in front because he doesn't understand it. But if he lets you do it because you believe in it, then at least you can get the culture started.

We were affecting 80 percent of the budget because the operations group here is everything. You could look at it and say the whole organization didn't want to make the change, but that didn't matter because you could at least start to make the change in the areas that affected the bottom line the most.

My promotion to president is going to raise some issues. Some people are going to end up leaving because they might not like my leadership or management style, but it will give me the opportunity to bring people in who believe the same thing. So slowly it's a culture change through education, attrition and bringing in new talent.

How important is it to get rid of the naysayers?
YUROVICH: Let me say it a different way. It's important to teach them, train them, teach them, train them, teach them, train them and if they don't want to be taught or trained, then have them make the right decision because it's very painful when you continually ask for them to change daily and they don't. It's perseverance. If you believe in your cause and can get everyone to believe in it and get excited about it, you'll win, but it's going to take time.

Did you get much resistance from people who thought it was too much of a change?
YUROVICH: There was a lot of resistance. People see that if they get really good somebody's job goes away. They believe that if they do it well, they're going to lose their overtime. You have all of the traditional self-preservation type of thoughts of the folks on the floor. But as we were able to do this, the core group of folks who have been here for a length of time have seen that their jobs have been made easier. They now have complete control of their respective areas. They have been given the tools plus the responsibility to move the product through the plant and meet the only thing that matters: the customer date and the customer order. These guys never got to see those tools. It was a mindless manufacturing work center.

There was an old supervisor mentality of work harder, work harder, work harder. But they were working hard on stuff they didn't need to ship.

Where are the current bottlenecks in the organization?
YUROVICH: I finally got a couple of our accounting folks to go to lean manufacturing for accountants because that is the traditional holdup.

How difficult is it to change from a batch and queue to a flow system of manufacturing?
YUROVICH: Whenever you walk out on the shop floor and look at a press that's not running, people initially think you're not paying for your investment and you're not working properly. We have set up an entire materials game plan through the plant and we are bringing suppliers in to explain to them where we are going and what we need them to do through kanbaning and deliveries.

It's important to teach them, train them, teach them, train them...

They were working hard on stuff they didn't need to ship.

What types of results have you seen since implementing lean?

YUROVICH: We have gone from a mediocre 4 to 5 percent operating income base to 12.5 to 13 percent last year. This is the only way we're going to stay competitive manufacturing in the Boston area because it's expensive.

Did you improve your margins in the late 1990s because of your new production system or because the economy was growing so well?

YUROVICH: We had more orders than we knew what to do with. We were very involved with late deliveries, so I spent a huge share of money — over seven figures — on expediting fees and keeping customers happy. So even though we had a heck of lot of orders — 20 percent higher than ever — we had over a million dollars of expediting fees that we would never of had to pay out prior, so it sort of offset itself. There were lots of natural highs and lows. In October of 1999, I had almost given up. Now we're really seeing some significant strides.

In October of 1999, I had almost given up...

What was necessary to overcome those lows?

YUROVICH: I was more of a dictator who had a vision. You have to believe it will work and then you have to convince people and train them on ways to take out waste. It forces you to think through the process and most folks you deal with don't want to sit down and think through the detail.

I was more of a dictator who had a vision.

Why? Is it because they don't have the time? Are they too busy?

YUROVICH: I think it comes down to being a Marine, being organized and understanding clearly the direction you want to take your organization. You may not be 100 percent correct, but if you're heading true north and everybody else is headed off a few degrees, at least you have the organization moving in a direction that will be favorable.

We like to work under a saying that 90 percent right today is better than 100 percent right six months from now. If people make mistakes here, which we do daily, we don't worry about it, but if we make the same one three or four times, then we have a problem because it proves that we're not smart enough to learn.

How important are consultants?

YUROVICH: We had an association with the Boston Manufacturing Association and the Kaizen Institute of America, but what it really came down to is each one of them had a different philosophy of how they attack it. You had to make your own game plan. What I tried to do with our team was to make a game plan that was non-intrusive as we seeded the ground. It took a lot of conflict resolution periods with our kaizen coordinator and supervisors. It took a lot of time to explain and sometimes I just had to say, here is how we're doing it and get on board or take a leap. For the most part, the folks who have tried it have realized over time that it's working and making their lives easier. They realize that the new guy isn't going to come in to try to get rid of them. Job security has been a key.

Are your customers demanding that you cut the prices of your products?
YUROVICH: They have and we have basically said no. It's a road to hell if you start to give up pricing especially when in the last four years we have not had a price increase with any of our customers.

It's a road to hell if you start to give up pricing.

Is there a great deal of discussion or analysis within your company of moving production to a low-labor-cost country?
YUROVICH: When you look at the labor rate across the nation, we're competitive and yet we are global. If you look forward 10 or 15 years, the cost of doing business in Taiwan or Mexico will catch up to Brighton and when that happens, you'll see a swing of manufacturing coming back to the United States because you'll get it locally and quicker.

What recommendations do you have for companies that are trying to pursue a lean strategy?
YUROVICH: It has to start from the top and they have to get buy-in from all of the executives of the organization. Second, people who get measured will respond to measurements. The third is training. Send as many folks as you have identified as key people to get formalized training and take that training and modify it to your organization.

What are some of your own lessons learned?
YUROVICH: You have to understand when to wield the big stick. But the real issue is measure, measure, measure. If you measure and get results, that's great. Sometimes you're going to measure and get bad results, but that is okay too.

THE BOEING COMPANY

It wasn't long ago that Boeing was in the throes of a financial crisis caused by clogged production lines and suppliers that could not keep up with a deluge of orders. Those problems have subsided, thanks in part to the widespread adoption of lean manufacturing throughout the company. Lean production is now written into Boeing's vision statement and lean principles are being studied and applied throughout the company.

Allen Haggerty is vice president and general manager of engineering for Boeing's Military Aircraft and Missile Systems Group and oversees lean engineering programs throughout Boeing. Jim Davis is director of the lean enterprise promotion office at Boeing.

We coined the term "lean engineering."

A value-stream analysis of the engineering function.

How hard it is to go from the Toyota Production System to Boeing?

HAGGERTY: We evolved our roadmap from the Toyota Production System. Over the last three years as I've looked [at Boeing's production] we've found that 80 percent of the product cost is determined in the early design stages. I felt that was one of the missing chunks so we coined the term "lean engineering."

In the Boeing definition, lean enterprise equals lean engineering plus lean suppliers plus lean manufacturing. We have a big focus on lean engineering and have established for all of our lean activities a capability maturity model, a CMM. This is similar to the software engineering enterprise capability maturity matrix which we use throughout industry and Department of Defense to rate software: level one, level two, three, four and five.

We measure ourselves against a similar matrix module on lean engineering. We think it is exclusive to the Boeing Company because nobody else has done that. We are just getting ready to start measuring how deep we've implemented lean engineering throughout the many divisions of the Boeing Company.

How much harder is it to adopt lean in the engineering arena as opposed to production where you can easily measure flow and takt time and the other lean principles?

HAGGERTY: It is absolutely more difficult. Processing a solid model or an engineering drawing involves design, stress, weights, aerodynamics and loads. One of the key elements of becoming lean in engineering is reducing the number of handoffs — the transactions and the interactions among the engineering groups related to manufacturing, tooling and NC programming.

We use a methodology that flow charts those operations and the number of handoffs and transactions. It says how can we co-locate people, minimize the handoffs, minimize the cycle time of those transactions by organizing our engineering activities for the maximum value added. It's a value-stream analysis of the engineering function that can in fact reduce waste and non-value added activities.

What do you do to get lean principles involved early in the design of an aircraft or complex military product?

HAGGERTY: Engineering up front controls over 80 percent of the cost because we are the ones who determine the number of parts, the tolerance of parts and the materials — whether it's going to be titanium or aluminum or graphite composite. We determine the processes, and very often we dictate the tooling concepts.

As a result of that, the manufacturing guys are classically less than 20 percent of the cost of the hands-on labor. We micromanage manufacturing with industrial engineered time standards and all sorts of inspection.

Our goal is to teach the engineers their impact on total product cost and value by getting them to use design for manufacturing and assembly; to reduce the number of parts; to use good techniques such as variation control, specifying the right kind of assembly and fabrication tolerances; and establishing robust processes. If engineering can turn over to the suppliers or factory the fewest number of parts with the most robust processes and tolerances that we know are going to fit the first time, we can reduce scrap and rework and downstream costs.

Manufacturing guys are classically less than 20 percent of the cost of the hands-on labor.

Some of the leading lean companies have questioned the role of the operator in a lean system — the guy on the shop floor— and in your case the engineer. How hard is it for you to address the role of the operator and engineer in a lean enterprise model?

HAGGERTY: One of the basic principles that we all learned from the Japanese model and the Toyota Production System — and as we have modified that and applied it into our U.S. culture — is standard work. The concept is to get the variability out of the work.

You can't ask the worker to do the job differently each time. Sometimes he has to do things differently because the parts don't fit. Well, that's an engineering, fabrication, quality or supplier goof.

When you have just-in-time parts, it's the world's greatest quality system because when the parts come just-in-time they have to be right. They have to fit and function exactly right.

Just-in-time parts is the world's greatest quality system...

We find there are dramatic savings in working with the operators and saying let's analyze the job and make sure the manufacturing work instructions are complete and comprehensive and understandable. We're using digital photography, putting those pictures into the computer and printing out the instructions. They have the bill of material, the pictures and the assembly sequence. They get a lot of pride in doing the job right the first time. So the operators are enthused about it.

We have a technique that we call accelerated improvement workshops, AIWs, which is our name for a kaizen event. We ran 90 or more of those in St. Louis and have run hundreds in the Military Aircraft and Missiles group last year and over 1,000 in the Space and Communications and Boeing Commercial groups last year. These are groups of 10 or so people who are in a manufacturing work cell or in a station on the assembly line or in the office environment doing software where the team learns the lean principles and between Monday and Friday brainstorms ways of improving the quality and cycle time, unit cost and inventory reduction.

Have the lean principles totally penetrated up and down the entire culture of Boeing?
HAGGERTY: Yes.

Are these principals known as lean or as something else?
HAGGERTY: It's known as lean enterprise. As part of the vision 2016, the Boeing Company has three core competencies: detailed customer knowledge and focus; large-scale systems integration; and lean and efficient design and production systems. You ask any executive of the Boeing Company including [CEO] Phil Condit and [President] Harry Stonecipher what the three core competencies of the Boeing Company are and they'll give you those.

In order for lean to work, you need to have buy-in from the very top, don't you?
HAGGERTY: It started there and it's been floating down.

You've got an acronym soup of software programs, such as Catia, ERP, SCM — supply chain management — and APS — advanced planning and scheduling. In the lean environment how do you wrestle with such problems associated with integration of all these software systems?
HAGGERTY: It is a major challenge getting our suppliers and fabrication and assembly shops to work under an integrated architecture. At the beginning of 1999, we appointed a common breakthrough systems software architect who has a staff of folks and we are integrating those modules.

Is the Catia design program the foundation of your lean engineering effort?
HAGGERTY: Today, with the heritage companies, Rockwell, McDonnell Douglas and Boeing, there were other design systems. The non-recurring bill to switch over immediately is cost prohibitive, so we have been able to develop outstanding translators. Our goal over time is to move to the Catia design environment completely.

The benefit of having common breakthrough systems whether they're aerodynamic loads, stress analysis, integrated logistics support or design systems is if you have a common design environment, the training, the software maintenance, the ability to move engineers among various locations or to move work packages via computer to other parts of the United States so you don't have to move people is much simplified. So we are moving to the Catia environment. Our concept is to be able to do work all over the world and make it fit.

A good example of that is the new 100-passenger Boeing 717. The

It is a major challenge getting our suppliers and fabrication and assembly shops to work under an integrated architecture.

tail of that aircraft comes from Taiwan; the nose comes from Korea; the wings come from a combination of Canada and Korea; the fuselage comes from Alenia in Italy; the engines come from BMW Rolls Royce in Germany. It's assembled in Long Beach. It's almost like a United Nations' airplane.

Not all of those manufacturers have one common design system but we have been able to do the necessary translations at the interface points and that airplane goes together very, very efficiently.

The big issue in manufacturing today is the fact that the OEMs are no longer manufacturers. Hewlett Packard and Cisco Systems contract all of their manufacturing out. Is that a model that Boeing is working toward?

HAGGERTY: Yes. Our concept of what we call moving up the value stream is identical to that. From a lean standpoint, when you do a value stream analysis and you look at the value analysis, there is not a heck of a lot of value the Boeing Company can add to a piece of sheet metal. There are small- and medium-sized shops with advanced NC sheet metal equipment that can produce that kind of high quality sheet metal part for us. Those shops do not have to be burdened with a tremendous research and development expense that we invest in to push the state of the art in every one of our product lines. That investment in R&D has to get burdened, accounting wise, into the cost of that sheet metal part. If those parts can be produced very efficiently by a small- to medium-sized company, then our concept is to move up the value chain to handle the stuff that mom- and pop-shops can't produce. We are putting our investment into those areas that provide leverage to us competitively.

Given your success with lean, is it worth buying out those mom- and pop-shops, lean out their processes and bring that production in-house?

HAGGERTY: Our lean supplier people send Accelerated Improvement Workshop kaizen event facilitators to our medium and small suppliers. The big guys know how to do this. We don't have to teach Pratt or B.F. Goodrich this kind of thing. We go to the small guys and we host seminars at our plant for three or four days and we bring them in and we teach them lean principles.

By providing the expertise and training, we can get the same leverage without having to buy those folks. We can buy those parts, they can be part of the supplier team, and we can get the benefit of competition.

How far along are you in propagating the lean concept through your supply chain?

HAGGERTY: We end up swapping best practices with the big guys. The little and medium guys take a while because there are literally thousands of them. We counted that there are over 30,000 suppliers to the

There is not a heck of a lot of value the Boeing Company can add to a piece of sheet metal.

Boeing Company. Our goal is to drive that down to below 18,000. For those guys who are left, we want them to move up the certification chain and we're trying to share with them the lean techniques.

I was in Tokyo in the early '90s and heard constantly that the U.S. aerospace sector was being targeted by Mitsubishi and others in Japan and that they had Boeing in their sights. Now you're using all of these Japanese lean production techniques.

HAGGERTY: One of the lessons we've learned from the Japanese is they have been very open in teaching the U.S. The reason Toyota says it's okay to teach us these techniques is because by the time we learn them, they're going to be two years ahead of us anyway.

We're using that technique.

I've been doing business in Asia for 20 years. The Korean, Taiwanese, Japanese and Indonesian aerospace industries are developing their first trainers, fighters and helicopters and they are doing very well.

Can those same factories build commercial airplane parts — build fighter assemblies and ultimately co-produce sections of the aircraft for us at the same time they are developing their own industry? Yes. Is it mutually beneficial to them? Yes. It is part of this global environment whereby we have to make the business relationships a win-win.

We are moving up that value chain so that we can move up to the system-of-systems concept and pulling together the disparate chunks for large-scale systems integration.

Is lean making a difference in Boeing's bottom line profitability?

HAGGERTY: As you reduce cycle time and achieve takt time and you move to just-in-time inventory, the inventory goes down and quality goes up. When you get the internal and external quality up, the rework and scrap costs go down. If you look at the income statement and balance sheet, as the quality goes up, the cost goes down. As the inventory goes down our return on net assets goes up and our cash flow goes up.

We are trying to blend together all of these islands of productivity. Some programs are much further along than others. Some are just starting, such as the clean-sheet-of-paper design of the factory in Alabama. They're starting off in a lean environment. We're getting to values of quality and cycle time and shop performance that we've never achieved before in many of our product lines.

We had some troubles a couple of years ago digesting a huge increase in commercial business. If you look at the 2000 annual report you can just see from the financial statements that the Boeing Company has its act together. It is dramatically impacting the good business performance of the Boeing Company. And it is just going to get better and better.

I heard that Pratt & Whitney president Karl Krapek was instrumental at getting Boeing involved in lean manufacturing. Is that true?

We are trying to blend together all of these islands of productivity.

HAGGERTY: Pratt & Whitney is a key supplier for us and we all witnessed the turnaround at Pratt. It was the first real aerospace achievement of a large company turnaround. Boeing Commercial had been evolving for about 10 years toward a lean manufacturing environment. We had taken numerous trips to Japan looking at Toyota, and Boeing does a lot of manufacturing there with Kawasaki and Mitsubishi.

Boeing had evolved towards it and had launched a very large program with Shingijutsu consulting firm to the point where the entire top management almost down to the middle management group was required to spend a week in Japan working on a production line with Shingijutsu.

The lean philosophy has accelerated.

Since the merger of Rockwell, McDonnell Douglas and Boeing in the summer of '96, that lean philosophy has accelerated and has been deployed across Space and Communications, Military Aircraft and Missiles and it continues to evolve in the commercial side.

Do you have some examples of lean successes?
HAGGERTY: The Boeing Company has constructed a greenfield site in Decatur, Ala., to produce the Delta 4 rocket as part of our initiative in space launch. Using the Shingijutsu consultants and our best lean folks, we changed the design of that plant while it was still on paper before the bulldozers ever got out there. The plant went from being three million square feet and 10 production lines to 1.5 million square feet and a moving production line. The payoff on lean goes from the complete conceptual design from how a factory should flow right to the end item point of use.

Is it much easier to do on a greenfield plant?
HAGGERTY: Certainly. But we have some great examples of just the opposite. We have a missile plant in St. Charles, Mo., where we build the Harpoon and the Conventional Air Launched Cruise Missile and the Joint Direct Attack Munition (JDAM). That plant has been there for 25 years, but when we won the JDAM contract we decided that we would take an old factory, clean it out and implement point-of-use, value-stream analysis and lean methodologies in every aspect of the plant. The trucks drive up to the loading dock and unload a plastic container that comes in from the suppliers with the key components in it.

The door to the factory opens up, which is five feet away from the loading dock, and that is position one on the assembly line and in four hours you have a JDAM missile. We are going up to production rates of 20,000 per year. This has been completely engineered to be a lean design, with lean suppliers with lean manufacturing in a total lean enterprise environment.

How long did it take you to produce one JDAM prior to the change?

HAGGERTY: Four months would have been great.

When you go into a plant do you say: "We're going to make this process lean and implement the five Ss and do everything that goes along with lean principles"?

HAGGERTY: The Spokane composite structures facility of Boeing Commercial used to produce all sorts of composites, flow beams and composite structures for exteriors and interiors. Their executive who runs that plant had gone to the Shingijutsu training.

Several years ago when Boeing made the commitment to increase its commercial production rate up to 41 aircraft per month for all models — 737, 747, 757, 767, 777 — they had determined that they were going to have to double the size of that plant with a significant amount of capital. When he came back from the lean training, he said, "We have an ideal opportunity to implement that here as we accelerate production and maybe we can avoid all of the expenditures on plant, equipment and personnel."

The facilities guys said you can't do that. We will stop five production lines unless we accelerate the construction of the planned expansion and go out and purchase all of the new autoclaves and ovens and other equipment that is needed.

The plant manager said you can fill out the capital asset requests but not submit them. He said if we get lean, we can accelerate and improve the output of this plant within the walls that we have. Everyone said it was high risk. They got the workforce and managers together and they ultimately implemented lean and put their workforce into manufacturing cells and they wound up staying inside the four walls. They only used half a million dollars of capital to make that production capacity increase. When they got done, as a gag, they had enough plant space to put a tennis court inside the factory. They painted white lines on the factory floor, put up a net and had guys play tennis inside just to show that they had tripled the production output and did it with their existing workforce.

If you minimize the waste, get the flow correctly and the takt time, you get the maximum utilization of the factory and human resources. You get everyone pulling together. You get point-of-use and just-in-time delivery. You get high quality. And you get rid of the waste that is involved in rework and scrap. You can do it in an existing factory.

You can do it in an existing factory.

Is that same production philosophy is going into improving all of Boeing's operations?

HAGGERTY: We've taken those commercial practices and have moved them into the Apache line at Mesa to the C-17 production line in Long Beach and the FA-18 production line and JDAM production line in St. Louis and St. Charles. We're deploying that to the CH-47 in Philadelphia. Our space folks in the production of our launch boosters are using it. We have a team of lean enterprise folks that are concentrating on the deployment of lean and we share best practices throughout the whole corporation.

How does the lean approach fit in with the problems with Milspecs and quality inspectors and the whole procurement system within Department of Defense? Is that a tough fit?

HAGGERTY: Our customers want lean because they are looking for affordability. DOD acquisition executives are pushing acquisition reform and a focus on affordability and they certainly applaud lean initiatives. The Air Force has funded the Lean Aerospace Initiative at MIT and the Lean Enterprise Model and as a result of that, lean principles are flowing down through the Department of Defense.

Have you seen a change in the number of military inspectors on your military production lines as a result of your lean implementations?

HAGGERTY: Yes. Our C-17 in Long Beach is a good example. As we have implemented our quality program and work toward ISO 9000 they've gone from 150 government inspectors on that line down to 18 now. The DCMC has recognized good quality and have backed off and that is a win-win situation for both industry and government.

Do your commercial customers place inspectors on Boeing's commercial lines?

HAGGERTY: Very, very few.

So they trust you?

HAGGERTY: Well, they trust the FAA system which is called Airworthiness Certification System Engineering Process. They come in with 20 or 30 inspectors every two to three years and look at every aspect of your business, including engineering, configuration management, drawing release and materials and processes. They go to the factory and procedures and handling of hazardous material and nonconforming parts and installation and assembly processes and make sure that people are trained and certified. Typically, an airline will have an engineering manager and a few inspectors at your plant. Depending on the size of the order, anywhere from two to five, certainly, not more than 10 people at a facility as opposed to hundreds which is classic in a military environment.

DAVIS: The Boeing goal is to have one Boeing company flight, one customer flight and then the third flight of the aircraft is a revenue flight. That is quite often met where the first flight has no problem. There is a designated customer rep that is a Boeing employee who does the walk-through on the aircraft and makes sure the paint is perfect. Many times the first time the customer sees the airplane is the first time they fly it.

How do you assure the lean philosophy is propagated throughout Boeing?

Our customers want lean because they are looking for affordability.

HAGGERTY: We have a facility called the Leadership Center in St. Louis. Personnel come from all over the corporation. It's a 2,800-acre facility on the Missouri River and it was a French chateau estate built in the '20s. We built a 160-bed residence facility.

Executives come for two weeks for the Boeing executive program. Middle managers come for a program called leading from the middle. All the new supervisors come to the facility.

It's patterned after the very successful General Electric facility in New York, where Jack Welch would take all of his top management and middle management. Harry Stonecipher, who is our chief operating office and president of Boeing, was a 26-year General Electric executive veteran and he felt we needed that.

We run a two-week class every month and then there are two one-week courses. Phil Condit our CEO and Harry Stonecipher, Debbie Hopkins our chief financial officer, and one of the three group presidents, Alan Mulally from Boeing Commercial, Mike Sears from Military Aircraft and Missiles and Jim Albaugh from Space and Communications attend and lecture once a month.

We get the top folks there. I teach the lean module with Norma Clayton who is our vice president of manufacturing and head of lean manufacturing. We spend a day as part of that two-week course on lean. Every executive, every vice president, every director that attends that session gets exposed to lean principles, lean thinking, lean applications and best practices.

How do you make sure your suppliers are adopting lean principles?

HAGGERTY: We have a really good program on supplier certification. We have gold, silver and bronze certified suppliers. To be a gold supplier it's something like 99 percent on-time delivery and very high quality, something like 99 percent. You have to have statistical process control implemented and perform to schedule, cost and quality. There are incentives in our contracting for folks to move from bronze to silver to gold.

As part of our total lean supplier effort, we have been able to reduce the number of total suppliers dramatically but increase the number of bronze, silver and gold certified suppliers.

As a result of having long-term relationships with those certified suppliers, we have found that our delivery performance has gone way up; the quality performance has gone way up; and our unit costs have come down because the guys are giving us parts that fit, parts delivered on time and parts we don't have to stock in large WIP inventory. Therefore, it's been a win-win. The benefit is long-term relationships and larger procurement buys.

What incentives do you have in place for workers to adopt lean practices and behavior?

> *Every executive, every vice president, every director that attends that session gets exposed to lean principles.*

The non-union people are tied to economic profit.

HAGGERTY: Debbie Hopkins our CFO has implemented this managing-for-value initiative where every executive and every member of management is focused on improving value for the Boeing company. We've always had an incentive compensation program now there is an employee performance incentive program where the total fortunes of the 200,000 people in the Boeing company, the non-union people, are tied to economic profit.

Economic profit is the parameter that everybody is going to read in the Boeing News every week. We'll be able to provide the salaried and non-union personnel up to two weeks pay by meeting and beating the economic profit incentive.

LEAN ACCOUNTING / BMA INC.

A lot has been written about companies adopting lean manufacturing techniques on the factory floor, but most implementations won't work unless the financial and accounting systems are in place to support the change.

Adopting a lean accounting system isn't particularly easy and there are not many tools available in the financial community to help.

"A lack of lean accounting, control and measurement will, inevitably, lead to the failure of the lean enterprise initiative because what is measured and accounted for are those issues the people within the company will focus their attention on," says Brian Maskell, president of BMA Inc., a lean accounting consulting firm based in Cherry Hill, N.J. Maskell has worked with numerous companies on implementing lean accounting systems including current work with Parker Hannifin Corp.

Traditional accounting systems are hostile to lean manufacturing.

As companies adopt lean manufacturing techniques are they becoming more acclimated to changing their accounting systems?

MASKELL: You don't have to get very far with lean manufacturing to find yourself hitting up against the problems with the traditional accounting control systems.

What are some of those problems?

MASKELL: Traditional accounting systems are hostile to lean manufacturing in that they motivate people to do non-lean things. For example, if we are taking traditional measures like efficiency and utilization and variance reporting, they are going to motivate people to just make more stuff in large batches to keep the machines running. Whereas in lean we're looking at the opposite — making today what the customer wants today.

Traditional accounting systems do not motivate people to lean behavior. In lean, we want to understand where the waste is and where the obstacles to flow are. If you look at a traditional accounting system, you won't find anything that will help you with that. In fact, it's the reverse. With standard costs, we actually hide waste from ourselves.

Do lean accounting methods disclose waste in the accounting process itself?

MASKELL: Traditional accounting systems are very wasteful in themselves with thousands and thousands of transactions associated with inventory control and production scheduling, shop floor controls, shop floor tracking, cost accounting and variance reporting. These thousands and thousands of transactions are not only wasteful, but they cause more waste because if you have a whole lot of transactions you have to produce reports. If you produce reports you're going to have meetings and then you're going to have reconciliations and all kinds of other stuff.

The issue here is why does a traditional company have all those transactions? The primary reason is that it is the only method the finance people have of maintaining financial control of the business. If you have processes that have a considerable amount of variability — and in most

Why does a traditional company have all those transactions?

There isn't the need for all the transactions.

cases processes are fundamentally out of control — then the only way to control them from a financial perspective is by checking and tracking and recording everything. When a company implements lean systems it is transforming processes that are fundamentally out of control and addressing the root cause of problems and bringing them under control.

As processes are brought under control, then increasingly there isn't the need for all the transactions.

But you just can't get rid of transactions. A lot of finance people rely on those transactions to do their job. What we're saying is eliminate transactions when you are satisfied that the processes are fundamentally under control and when they are no longer needed to provide financial or operational control of the business.

Does this lead to a power struggle in most companies between the production people and the finance people?

MASKELL: It can if there is not an understanding. That is why lean accounting needs to become just another tool of lean thinking. Very often companies just plunge into lean manufacturing without understanding the financial implications of what they are doing. When that happens, the operational people are very happy with themselves because they've done wonderful lean things.

But the effect on the bottom line is usually that there is no effect or very often it shows that things are going in the wrong direction. It is not at all uncommon for profitability to go down in the early stages of lean manufacturing.

What causes the profitability to go down in the short term is the elimination of inventory.

Is that a function of not being able to measure the right things?

MASKELL: Mostly what causes the profitability to go down in the short term is the elimination of inventory. If you significantly pull out large amounts of finished goods and work-in-process inventory, then you will be posting a significant amount of cost to the cost of sales for that month. Surprisingly, many companies don't understand that. It comes as a shock and that is when there can be conflict.

The conflict comes for two reasons. First the finance people haven't been involved in the changes to the way that they should have been and second they don't have good tools for assessing the financial implications of what is happening when the transition is made to lean. Traditional accounting methods were developed to support mass production and the underlying assumptions of that system are different from the underlying assumptions of lean.

Do financial people ever lead or spearhead a lean initiative?

MASKELL: We've frequently seen controllers and CFOs who tell their operations people that when they get their cycle time down from two weeks to three days they're going to pull out all of their transactions. Often times, the real waste is in the processes that support production

ERP is largely irrelevant to lean.

within production planning and scheduling, cost accounting, the inventory control system and the shop-floor control system.

Have the financial software programs like ERP and now supply chain management systems hindered or helped the conversion toward lean? Have they provided the tools people need for this transition to a lean accounting system or have they made it harder?

MASKELL: ERP is largely irrelevant to lean. I often get asked the question, "What is the best software we should be using for the lean environment?" The answer is the one you've got because it's already paid for. We typically remove the more sophisticated functionality of a company's accounting software system. A simpler system helps. Supply chain management is a different story because that can be helpful in integrating the supply chain.

How hard is it to take the financial systems and reconfigure them to lean?

MASKELL: It's not easy because these systems are very much imbedded in the structure of the company. It's like pulling out crab grass, the roots grow very deep.

Is better to take a "Roundup" type of approach and start with an entirely new accounting system?

MASKELL: Doing lean and ERP at the same time is impossible because it takes the same people. If a company only has a certain number of people with the right kind of skills you can't have half of them working on one thing and the other half working on another. I always say address the lean issues first because then the ERP implementation will be a lot simpler.

Lean accounting works by value stream.

Is it self evident which transactions get eliminated?

MASKELL: Lean accounting works by value stream. People identify the transactions and the reasons for them. You must determine what needs to be in place in order to remove those transactions while still maintaining control of the business. If we want to eliminate work-in-process tracking, we have to have inventory levels of work in process that have to be relatively low and consistent. Relatively low means the production cycle time needs to be short, and consistent means there has to be some sort of kanban or pull system that is really working, is effective and people are maintaining the rules. There have to be performance measurements in place to ensure that the kanban system is working right.

What are key issues for implementing lean accounting methods?

MASKELL: These change for companies over time depending on where they are in the conversion. A key one is performance measures in all the processes of the value stream, at both the cell level and the administrative or non-production process level as well.

There is also the need for measures at a corporate or division level that determine whether the strategy of the business is being achieved. You don't just make these measures up; you start off with the business strategy and then you create a linkage of the measures from the business strategy through to the corporate or division-level measures.

From that we develop the continuous improvement measures at the value-stream level and from that we'd be looking to see what each element of the value stream, each cell or each process, contributes to the achievement of the value-stream measures. Those are then rolled down to the specific measures at the cell level.

What are some examples of measures needed at the production level?

MASKELL: There have to be a handful of measures that are really focused on helping people achieve today what they have to do today. We need a by-the-hour report that is tracking whether we are making to cycle time and achieving it.

We're interested in dock-to-dock time because that is a measure of flow. How long does it take from the time material comes in to the time it gets shipped out in the form of a product? Some people think of that as lead time, but it's different from lead time, it's measuring flow of the process.

The purpose of value stream measures is to create continuous improvement. We need five or six measures; most companies have too many measures that are focused on the value stream.

What are you trying to measure on a corporate-wide scale?

MASKELL: A key issue is the calculation of the financial benefits of lean manufacturing. A lot of companies start with lean manufacturing from an operational perspective. The finance person is usually not too involved and quite rightly asks, "Where is it hitting the bottom line? I'm not seeing any improvement. There is all this activity going on and all this self-congratulation on what we've achieved, but where is the beef?"

All the measures in the traditional accounting system will be showing red lights with things that are going wrong and bad. The company will not be absorbing overhead capacity. Labor variances will show underutilization.

The finance people need different tools for understanding the benefits of lean manufacturing and very often it takes time for those financial benefits to manifest themselves.

If a company is really committed to a lean conversion, how long will it take to start showing positive financial returns?

MASKELL: People think of lean manufacturing as being another cost-cutting method, but we're taking processes, removing waste and cre-

We need a by-the-hour report that is tracking whether we are making to cycle time and achieving it.

All the measures in the traditional accounting system will be showing red lights...

ating new capacity. As you take the waste out, you are creating available capacity and the financial benefit depends entirely on what you do with that available capacity. If you're in the good situation where you can sell more than you can currently make, then you're going to get benefit in the short term. With more capacity, you'll make more product and make more revenue. Other companies go exactly the other way. They take that capacity and lay it off. That is not the optimum, but they are significantly overstaffed.

With more capacity, you'll make more product and make more revenue.

Most companies take time before their additional capacity can begin to reflect increased revenues so there needs to be a good understanding of how that additional capacity is used. We've developed tools for taking the value-stream maps and understanding from a financial perspective what additional resources are freed up and how they are used so the financial benefits can become clear. Those usually require some strategic decision making.

But aren't there immediate financial benefits to reducing inventory?

MASKELL: Transactions are to lean accounting what inventory is to lean manufacturing. All transactions are waste. In lean manufacturing, we hate inventory and the reason for that is because we hold inventory when there are problems that have not been solved. We hold raw materials because our suppliers don't supply on time or quality is not very good or we don't know how to order the right things at the right time or because your supplier is in China and it takes weeks to get there. We hold that inventory because we know there are obstacles to flow that haven't been eliminated. The same is true of transactions that are there because the processes are not yet under control.

Can you lean out all the transactions from a traditional manufacturer?

MASKELL: Pretty much. But even when you go to the world's best walk-on-water lean companies there is still inventory because there are problems they haven't yet solved. The same would be true with transactions. Theoretically we can more or less eliminate all transactions, but in reality it's a step-by-step process.

Companies have to eliminate standard costing altogether...

As companies move down the lean implementation path, do other accounting obstacles become prevalent?

MASKELL: Companies have to eliminate standard costing altogether and replace it with the simpler method of value-stream costing. We say there should be no allocations of overhead. The allocation of overhead gets in the way and becomes complicated. Lean companies have developed methods to eliminate pretty much all of the allocation by addressing costs at the value-stream level. This enables them to collect cost information in summary form very simply. We don't have to track labor, we know what the labor cost of the value stream is because we can get it from the payroll. We don't need to track the inventory we've got because it's low and consistent. We know what we're buying. If you use what you buy quickly there is no need to keep track of where it is and what the costs are.

You grow into these things. We're not suddenly saying stop with the inventory tracking, cut it all out, but as you become more mature with lean manufacturing, you can eliminate most of the standard costing and replace it with something that is better.

Is there an overriding philosophy for lean accounting?

MASKELL: We're really focused on creating more value for the customer, whereas traditional accounting is much more concerned with cutting costs. But that doesn't mean that cost is unimportant.

Do the financial tools exist to keep track of value-stream costs?

MASKELL: It is simple enough so that you can do this with spreadsheets or an ERP system by switching off most of the things in the ERP system that aren't necessary to gather these costs around value streams. Many companies go on to reorganize themselves around value streams and then begin to collect costs by value stream. That is just part of the lean process.

That brings you to target costing, which is for more sophisticated lean companies that are trying to understand the value that they're creating for the customer. They need to understand what it is they do that creates that value in terms of product, processes and services and drive that value back through the business.

Are manufacturing companies that have gotten to this level doing better than those that haven't?

MASKELL: It's mixed. There are a lot of very good car companies that run ads for year-end close out sales. That means they're overstocked. We have a client that is a wonderful lean manufacturer, but they're in the telecom industry and they're in terrible shape. They have a new product they've been working on for months and their customers have said they don't want it.

People make the analogy of a healthy person. If someone is overweight and drinks too much and doesn't exercise then when something bad happens like they have an accident or they get attacked by a virus or they have a strain on their heart, they are unlikely to be able to handle it. Whereas people who are reasonably healthy and have taken care of themselves are more likely to bounce back.

But healthy people get bad diseases and drop dead too. So I don't think being lean is any guarantee that the slings and arrows of outrageous fortune are going to pass you by.

Are the business schools teaching lean accounting methods to accounting and finance majors?

MASKELL: Right now, the problem is that there are not that many

> *We're focused on creating more value for the customer, whereas traditional accounting is much more concerned with cutting costs.*

> *Healthy people get bad diseases and drop dead too.*

This is not radical new stuff.

people who are trained and experienced in lean accounting. There aren't textbooks on it. There are a few books out of Japan, and there is quite a bit of research going on in the performance measurement area. But not much is being taught.

But I don't want to paint the picture that this is radical new stuff in that we don't implement anything that isn't in the textbooks somewhere. It's just that we're applying it from a lean perspective. When we talk about value-stream costs, what we're really doing is direct process costing. The same would go with transactions.

If companies adopt lean accounting systems do they reduce their payroll within their accounting departments?

MASKELL: Not really. The accounting person in the average company spends about 70 percent of their time on routine bookkeeping and reporting activities and they want to eliminate large chunks of that and free up their capacity. The finance people need to join the value stream team and be part of the continuous improvement management of the value stream using the analytical skills they've developed for the improvement of the value stream. Most finance people love it when it happens.

Who has the ear of the CEO? The production guy or the finance guy?

MASKELL: Some people assume that the finance people are naturally more conservative than the operations people and that's not been my experience.

Problems With Traditional Costing Systems In A Lean Enterprise:

- Provides no useful improvement information.
- Leads production people to do the wrong things: large batches; build inventory; build ahead and "earn" hours.
- Hides waste by lumping into overhead and other factors.
- Organized by departments and not by value stream.
- Provides no useful information for managers and executives to plan cost reductions and improvements.
- Creates waste through transaction-laden system.

Principles of Lean Management Accounting:

- Manage by value streams.
- Constantly identify waste.
- Make everybody accountable for cost reduction at their own level.

- All reporting is linked to improvement cycles.
- Accounting people are primarily change agents integrated with operations teams.
- Consistent and coherent rollup of cost and performance reports by value stream, program, company and sector.
- Accounting control and measurement systems must themselves be lean.

Cell Measurements In Lean Manufacturing

- Measurements must address the principles of lean thinking: value; value stream; flow; pull; perfection.
- There must be a few focused and relevant measurements.
- Measurements are designed to assist the value stream owner to control and improve the cell.
- Measurements must be real time and "pulled" when they are needed.

ARMY MATERIEL COMMAND

The lean manufacturing philosophy of value-stream analysis, continuous improvement and elimination of waste is taking a foothold in an unlikely organization — the U.S. Army.

The 50,000-employee Army Materiel Command (AMC), which runs five large industrial depots, the Army Research Lab, logistics operations and major arsenals and ammunition plants throughout the world, has adopted lean production as one of its core missions, thanks to the enlightenment of its Commander General Paul Kern and a grass-roots effort to implement lean techniques in the field.

Lean manufacturing plays a prominent role in the AMC Strategy for transformation. It is there primarily because Kern read the book *Lean Thinking*, saw what lean could do in real-life applications, and decided that he would lead the charge. Kern has organized lean training sessions for his senior executive staff at headquarters and general officers in all of AMC's subordinate commands. He will institute lean training throughout the entire breadth of the organization.

"We will conduct training on a recurring basis to promulgate this throughout the command and get it to the lowest echelon and sustain the momentum of lean thinking across the command," says Col. Robert Chadwick, the General's staff group director in charge of the effort at headquarters in Alexandria, Va.

The plan is to take lean concepts into the production processes in the field, achieve and publicize successes, broaden the program, develop lean champions and move it beyond the shop floor into administrative and logistics functions. "We're getting the senior leadership excited about its potential and at the employee level there is success," says Chadwick. "So there is a lot more ownership than if it had been dictated from on high."

AMC runs industrial operations in aviation, automotive, communications, electronics, chem-bio, missiles and repair and overhaul. It produces ammunition and provides operational support to warfighters. Most of its industrial base was built during World War II. The command believes there is a good fit between an integrated lean manufacturing operation and the fast-developing all-digital Army.

"Gen. Kern is not approaching this like it's the latest management fad," says Chadwick. "He's not going to sprinkle it on a few PowerPoint charts and present it at the next conference. He'll hold his leadership accountable. He'll resource it. He'll educate and train people to carry out his vision. He will reward it and incentivize it in the organization. We will want our metrics to capture the results of these initiatives and efforts to know if we're getting a return on our investment. He's prepared to lead it in addition to manage the process."

It did not take a directive from headquarters for one Army maintenance depot located 18 miles west of Texarkana, Texas, to begin an aggressive implementation of lean manufacturing. In fact, it took the 9/11 terrorist attack for an Army reserve officer who had experience in lean in the private sector to be reactivated for duty at the Red River Depot.

After surveying the industrial operations at Red River, Lt. Dave Meyer — now elevated to the rank of captain — said there was a better way to do things. His observations and perseverance on how lean could transform the depot caught the attention of Red River Commander Lt. Col. Fred Hart.

Hart then read the book *Lean Thinking*, heard about the lean initiative taking place at the Warner Robins Air Force Base in Georgia, hired the Simpler Consulting firm under an existing Air Force contract and went to work on training the 1,400 people in the depot.

Red River has an operating budget of $230 million. It runs 17 production programs involving vehicles, engines and components. It remanufactures 590 vehicles per year under a "recapitalization" program in which it fully refurbishes 20-year-old heavy combat and tactical vehicles to make them like new — zero miles, zero hours.

After Hart got the ball rolling at Red River, Army Materiel Commander Paul Kern from headquarters visited the complex and shortly thereafter issued his proclamation to implement lean throughout the entire Army Materiel Command.

Why has your depot adopted lean manufacturing?

HART: Because it's a program that can save a depot. Depots have been here about 60 years and we really have not stayed in touch with how industry has moved to more efficient ways of production. We came across lean from the Warner-Robins Air Force Base. We went there and talked to the workforce, which mirrors our workforce, and made the assessment that if it can work at an Air Force depot it can certainly work at an Army depot.

We're starting off in the crawl-walk-run stage. We took it upon ourselves to implement lean in our re-capitalization program for vehicles used by combat engineers in the field to see if we could help save money and improve the production flow. We are also leaning various other shops where the axles and engines are done and the cabs rebuilt. We want to lean that whole process from the front door to the back door.

Is it cheaper to rebuild a vehicle from the ground up than it is to buy a new one from a contractor?

HART: The subcontractors and OEMs that used to produce them are no longer around or are no longer tooled to do it. They say, "If you want us to build a whole new fleet of combat engineer vehicles, we'll charge you a good price." The Army costed it all out and we basically can provide a like-new product for roughly half the price.

What are your immediate goals with your lean implementation?

HART: Our goal is to drive the recapitalization cost down by 10 percent each year until we have eliminated all waste and gotten as close as we can to perfection. It's a big challenge for the government because we have a tendency to be wasteful, but lean brings a new perspective and a new rigor to the process. We're really excited about it.

Does the lean philosophy of empowering workers fit into the military command-and-control mentality?

HART: I think it does. I have been in the service for about 27 years and early on in our shop operations and motor pools we used the idea of 5-S. We would inspect to those kinds of standards, but over the years we've gotten away from it.

The military after World War II set the trends and industry used to come to the services to look at how we were organized. But through the Cold War, we became sluggish, very large and bureaucratic and we never broke out of that. Even though it's been over 10 years since the end of the Cold War, we're all still trying to shed a lot of that legacy bureaucracy.

So I would tell you we used to do lean, but it wasn't called lean in those days. We used to focus on having everything in its place, now it's just you put all kinds of tools and equipment on the floor and they aren't used and they accumulate. There is no rigor in the system.

We're starting off in the crawl-walk-run stage.

We became sluggish, very large and bureaucratic and we never broke out of that.

Have you assessed the benefits to adopting lean?

HART: The nice thing that lean has brought to this depot is the value-stream mapping and analyzing our process. The Army is big on process — how do you get from A to B to C. But we've never looked at it in our industrial base and that is what is great with lean. It's putting the discipline of reviewing the process back into our industrial base.

For instance, how do we integrate with the Defense Logistics Agency for parts? How do we integrate with the OEMs for technical support for parts? The value-stream mapping brings all that to light.

At Red River, all the production facilities were built 60 years ago and they were based on the batch-and-queue-process. We're finding that with lean we're finally moving things around on our production line so that we have the blasting and the cleaning and painting co-located to eliminate the travel of parts. We had bumpers and axles that would leave the production line two or three times to go out and be painted. Brakes would leave the production line to be specced.

On the combat engineer vehicle, we found the engine came and went from the production line a few times. The axles came and went. Now we've co-located the engine shop and the axle production shop along the production line so it all feeds into a one-piece flow. It's been monumental.

Did the Army Materiel Command adopt lean based upon your experience?

HART: I would like to give Red River the credit. There is no doubt and no argument that we were the first Army depot to implement this program. When Gen. Kern at AMC visited us in the spring we briefed him on our plans. Ever since then, he's had folks come down to look at it. So I'd like to say Red River got the ball rolling, bringing it to the attention of the Army Materiel Command.

What do you do next?

HART: We put together a planning cell of 10 people called the Red River Production System team and they're just now putting the plan together with milestones targeting each area. We're putting together a schedule and over the course of the next five years we'll start the process. We have about 12 rapid improvement events scheduled this year and we've completed seven.

A lot of folks think you can read the book *Lean Thinking* or attend a seminar, learn some of the lingo and then go back and apply it to your operation. I will just tell you at a U.S. Army depot, you have got to have a sensei, a mentor down here. So we hired Simpler [Consultants]. If you're left to your own devices to do it, you can't do it because the commander, who is me in my case, can't spend the amount of time necessary to be the change agent on the floor. The duties and responsibilities that the commanding officer has here means you're on the road regularly.

So a sensei like Simpler gives you the focus to keep you on track and

We're finally moving things around on our production line.

If you're left to your own devices to do it, you can't do it.

provides the coaching and mentoring that you need to keep the process going. You have to keep someone like them involved because it forces the depots into maintaining some rigor in the system and not allow it to fall by the wayside.

We have an older workforce and turnover is a fact of life. It's a constant training process to bring on new people. You train the workforce on it and then you have to have someone prepared to step up and be that next supervisor. It's a challenge.

Do you think lean is going to be tough to institutionalize?

HART: Once they start seeing the tangible savings and benefits and efficiencies, I think it will catch on. I will tell you I think this will eventually spread to the tactical Army in the field units because we want to lighten the logistics tail that has to support our combat troops. You can do a value-stream map as part of your mission analysis and it can help you lean how much stuff you have on airplanes and ships that is going to the warfighter. With the current philosophy in DOD, I think there is going to be a hard push to get this ingrained.

We've heard so much about the military's revolution in business affairs, but efforts to improve efficiency within the military seem to peter out every few years. Will the same fate hold true for lean?

HART: What I like about lean is the grass roots buy-in. Change imposed is change opposed. With lean, you don't come in and impose the change on the workforce. You tell them that we'll provide the resources, the time, the tools and you tell us what's the smart way of doing this. What makes good sense? How should it flow? How should it be set up? You get that buy-in.

Once you get that buy-in on the grass roots level, the tough nut is to get the buy-in at the management level. That's been our experience here. I've got shop floor workers coming up saying — "Hey Colonel, I know we're doing a rapid improvement event in August, but we're already looking at how we can make this better now." So it's getting to be contagious.

Is there another business or production system you've seen in your career that has the potential for such an impact?

HART: No. There have been a lot of initiatives over the years, but nothing like this. It dovetails in with the current initiative with the chief of staff of the Army which is called Army Transformation, which is the notion of making our fighting force lean and mean and ready to go. I would tell you that for the Army industrial base I think lean is a viable solution to achieve the end state that the senior leaders of the Army are looking for. It's great stuff; we love it.

What will create the ignition point throughout the Army?

This will eventually spread to the tactical Army in the field units.

Change imposed is change opposed.

It's getting to be contagious.

HART: As I told the workforce here, you're either making dust or eating dust. People are going to look at you and determine if you're making dust — in other words are you moving out with lean and do you have the metrics to show the improvements, the savings and so forth? I think they'll accomplish that, but the skeptics inside the Beltway will want to see the proof. That's going to be the challenge, which is to implement lean and be able to document the efficiencies that we're getting out of it.

There have been skeptics who say you're getting things cleaned up and all your tools are in the right place, but are you really saving anything? Right now, our savings are identified on paper because we're just in the infancy with it, but I think it will come to fruition in the next 12 to 18 months and then the Army will say this is powerful stuff.

The Army will say this is powerful stuff.

What are your initial goals?

HART: The goal is 10 percent improvement and I think that is going to be an easy target to achieve. If we come out in the black at the end of the fiscal year, we can do bonus payouts to the workforce, so lean will help them drive toward achieving those bonus payouts.

What would you recommend for other depots?

HART: You need to read *Lean Thinking*, then find yourself a firm like Simpler that is on site on the ground and part of your team. If you think you can read the book and attend the seminar and do it yourself, you won't achieve it. You have to hire experienced mentors who have truly walked the walk — been in an organization that has implemented it and worked in the production area. There are too many white-collar contractors who might come in who've read the books and taken some training courses, but when they get in front of wage-grade mechanics and production workers and are talking to them about how they can improve their process, if they don't understand manufacturing and production processing, those workers won't have any faith in you. My worker bees who have been through it have to say these guys know what they're talking about — I can tell they have worked on shop floors before. They know because all shop floors are basically the same.

How important was the base closure threat to propelling you into this?

If you're not efficient, you've got to justify your existence.

HART: That was the big motivator. One of the principles of lean is to find something to grab onto as a reason for doing lean, and that was our reason. The DOD BRAC initiative is now called the Efficient Facilities Initiative. That tells you something right there. This time around, the press release says if you're not efficient, you're suspect and you've got to justify your existence or we're going to chop you. So we looked at it and said, "Hey, lean will help us be efficient." So the goal here is to make a compelling case that we're the most efficient of the Army's five depots. I said, "Folks, we have to come out on top of this thing."

I have tried to remain relentless keeping people focused on it.

Since you are leaving your post, is your successor going to be an effective change agent? Is this a problem with the military moving people in and out?

HART: It can be, but my deputy and I did a battle handoff a few months ago. He's a civilian so he is the continuity here. He picked up the mantle to be the lean change agent along with a couple of other folks down the line. My replacement has been on board transitioning with me and there is no doubt in my mind that he is a big believer in this too. I have tried to remain relentless keeping people focused on it.

ANDON: Lights or display boards on or above a production line that indicate normal and abnormal running conditions.

CELLULARIZATION: The placement of machines in coherent groups to foster the flow of materials through an efficient sequence.

CHAKU-CHAKU: Means load - load in Japanese. Allows an operator working in a flow environment to load pieces from one machine to the next.

CHANGEOVER: The amount of time it takes to set up a machine from producing one product to another including the time it takes to make all necessary adjustments and inspections.

CYCLE TIME: The amount of time it takes an operator to conduct one cycle of an operation.

DMAIC: Design, Measure, Analyze, Improve and Control. A system of continuous improvement.

5-S: Cleaning up the factory or workspace so that it is spotless. It means to:
- Sort tools and remove all unnecessary items from the work space (Seiri);
- Store, arrange and label items so they are easily found (Seiton) ;
- Shine or clean everything so that an abnormal condition can be easily spotted (Seiso);
- Standardize the process of sorting, storing and shining every day (Seiketsu);
- Sustain the process by institutionalizing 5-S (Shitsuke).

FIVE WHYS: Analyzing a problem by asking "Why?" five times.

FLOW: An ideal production system in which one piece flows through a plant from one value-added step to the next with no waste, unnecessary inventory, delays or quality breakdowns.

FMEA: Failure Mode and Effect Analysis — Identifying potential failures and the source of potential failures and taking action to avoid them from happening.

HEIJUNKA: Leveling production in a plant.

JIDOKA: Programming machines to identify defects and abnormal conditions.

JUST-IN-TIME: Making products in quantities exactly when they are needed. The strategy exposes waste and makes continuous improvement possible.

KAIZEN: Continuous improvement. In Japanese it means "good change."

KANBAN: Communicating the need for materials or pieces through the use of signals or cards.

KPI: Key Performance Indicator.

MUDA: Means waste in Japanese — waste from overproduction, waiting, unnecessary transportation, inefficient processes, unnecessary inventory, unnecessary motion, producing defective goods and unused creativity.

MURA: Unevenness.

MURI: Unreasonableness.

NOISE: Conditions that cannot easily be controlled and are generally not worth worrying about.

ONE-PIECE FLOW: Producing one piece at a time, from raw material to finished product.

PARETO CHART: A statistical method of determining the important factors in an operation that are worth addressing and excluding the majority of other factors that inconsequential. It is also known as the 80-20 rule.

POKA-YOKE: Mistake-proofing a production system.

PRODUCTION SMOOTHING: Adapting production to variable demand to efficiently utilize material, labor, equipment and space.

PULL: Producing a product only when the customer orders it or wants it.

QUALITY AT THE SOURCE: Means a production system that can immediately respond to abnormalities; prevents the recurrence of abnormalities; gives equipment the ability to sense when it is producing defects and stop, and never passes defects to the next operation.

SINGLE-PIECE FLOW: Each complete product proceeds through design, order-taking and production without interruptions, back flows or scrap.

SIX SIGMA: A defect rate of 3.4 parts per million (ppm). Five sigma is 233 ppm; four sigma is 6,200 ppm; three sigma is 66,803 ppm; and two sigma is 308,733 ppm.

SMED: Single Minute Exchange of Dies. The goal is to changeover production equipment in less than 10 minutes.

STANDARD WORK: Provides a detailed guide to the activities of individual workers in the production environment. It includes all aspects of the the job including the takt time, sequence of motion, inventory and tasks performed.

TAKT: A German term that refers to tempo or beat. TAKT time equals available minutes in a shift divided by the customer demand for that shift.

TARGET COSTING: Estimating the cost of a product during its design phase.

3-P: Production Preparation Process — The design of an optimum production system that minimizes quality defects and all costs associated with a new product.

TPM: Total Productive Maintenance is carried out on every piece of equipment by all those who work on it with a goal of substantially reducing or eliminating equipment failure or downtime.

VALUE STREAM: The activities that add value during the creation production and delivery of a product.

VISUAL CONTROL: A production system in which everything is apparent to anybody looking at it.

WIP: Work in Process — inventory.

QUICK ORDER FORM

PLEASE SEND ME A COPY OF

Lean Machines: Learning From The Leaders Of The Next Industrial Revolution

- ❏ $69.00
- ❏ $59.00 each for two copies.
- ❏ $49.00 each for three or more copies.

Indicate number of copies here: _____

(Please add 4.5 percent sales tax for products shipped to Virginia addresses.)

Postage & Shipping: $6.00   Total Amount: _____

Payment options:

❏ Check enclosed   *Make checks payable to Publishers and Producers. (Our Federal Tax ID No. is 54-171-0088.)*

❏ Charge my: ❏ VISA   ❏ MC   ❏ AMEX

Account No. _____ Exp. _____/_____

Signature _____

SHIP TO:

NAME _____

ORGANIZATION _____

ADDRESS _____

CITY/STATE _____ ZIP _____

PHONE _____

E-MAIL (Optional) _____

Fax Orders: 703-750-0064
Telephone Orders: 703-750-2664
E-Mail Orders: orders@manufacturingnews.com
Postal Orders: Publishers & Producers, P.O. Box 36, Annandale, VA 22003
Order Online At: http://www.manufacturingnews.com

PUBLISHERS & PRODUCERS

http://www.manufacturingnews.com